an
ANGEL
for
every
day

an
ANGEL
for
every
day
Angela
McGerr

Illustrations by Richard Rockwood

Quadrille

This book furthers your journey on the angelic Way of Love and Light, the way of the open heart. As you work with the angels and unconditional love, you allow water of life to pour into the chalice of your heart. As your heart flower opens and unfolds to radiate love and beauty around you, you have truly moved far along the Way.

Other works by Angela McGerr:

A Harmony of Angels

Harmony Angel Cards

Angelic Abundance

Gold & Silver Guardian Angels

This paperback edition first published in 2007 by Quadrille Publishing Limited
Alhambra House, 27–31 Charing Cross Road, London WC2H OLS

Project editor Anne Furniss
Editor Nicki Marshall
Design Ros Holder
Production Rebecca Short

British Library Cataloguing in Publication Data
A catalogue record for this book is available from the British Library

ISBN: 978 184400 498 0

Printed and bound in China

Contents

Introducing the angelic year

The purpose of this book

This book helps you to draw on the loving support of angels by inviting them into your life, as I do, every single day. As you learn to work with angelic energy, day by day, month by month, you will gradually find that all the names of the angels and their special roles become second nature to you. You will be encouraged to rethink your views about what is possible and impossible in life, as the angels help you to deal more easily with the stresses and strains of today's world.

Angel aid for karmic issues

We must all face the fact that certain challenges are given to us for a reason. Having the benefit of angelic support helps you to turn some of life's negatives into positives. If you can learn to accept and move on through the lessons of life, your heart will start to feel more peaceful and contented, gradually providing a core of calmness.

How to use this book

Those who have read *A Harmony of Angels* will know that you can start this philosophy by invoking the ruling seven angels of the days of the week on their special days. In this book, covering the twelve months of the year, we build on this knowledge by working with the zodiac angels who govern these months. You might want to dip into the book for just a page when you have a crisis to deal with; you could choose to follow the suggestions for a whole month (perhaps your birth month, or the month you buy or are reading the book); or you might decide to follow each chapter systematically for the entire year.

The book's structure

The book is structured into twelve chapters covering the months from January to December, each being complete in itself. You could open it entirely at random and see what the angels would like to tell you through that page, as it is certain to be relevant to your life. Or you might start with the chapter on your own zodiac angel, as the issues are sure to be familiar to you. Another way is to begin at the time of year in which you acquire this book, looking to see how the advice of the angels of that month can assist – the choice is yours!

A *typical chapter*

Chapter One covers December to January and the zodiac sign Capricorn, whose ruler is the angel Nadiel. This is an earth sign ruled by Saturn. Capricorn typically features the following attributes, for which the angels offer assistance in the chapter:

Confidence, inner conviction, practicality
Thoroughness, determination, staying power

It may be that you have just the right blend of these qualities, or you could have too much or too little of one of them. The angels of the chapter help you to achieve a balance.

Capricorn is an earth sign; the elemental angels are involved in each chapter and in this chapter they offer these earth strengths:

Inner strength, wisdom and calmness
Growth and expansion of positive emotions

Once again, if you feel you need any of these strengths, this chapter will help.

Each zodiac sign is ruled by one of the planets in the solar system. Capricorn is ruled by Saturn; Saturn's ruler is the angel Cassiel, who can influence:

Your ability to embrace change and/or conquer challenges

If you have been facing, or are about to face challenges, then Cassiel offers a meditation to come to terms with this and move on in life.

Using the book with the Harmony Angel Cards

The Harmony Angel Cards introduce the concept of working with the zodiac angels, and this book can be used in conjunction with a card drawn from the Star Fire suit of Pistis Sophia. Following a reading that includes a card from this suit, you would have a message from one of the zodiac angels about personality issues you need to tackle. You can now go to this angel's chapter in this book and use it as a practical aid to addressing this message.

Making angelic invocations a daily practice

It is recommended that you work with your chosen angels every day in various ways. The first thing to learn is how to actually call in (invoke) angel energy, for angels will always come if you are calling on them from your heart. It's true that you would increase both energy and focus if you were able to work with your personality issues in the actual month in which they are specifically featured. However, you can (and I do) call on them all the time, wherever you are, whatever you are doing – on a walk, in the bus, car or office, or standing in your kitchen.

At the beginning of each chapter, you are told how to make the invocations. They are all really easy to do and memorise, enabling you to repeat them daily or when necessary. There are also simple exercises and meditations to build up your angelic connection. (If you would like more detailed information on or channeling from any of the angels in this book, this can be found in the *Book of Angels* within the Gold & Silver Guardian Angels pack.)

Changing your life

For life-changing angelic help you are recommended to start where you like in the book but progress through all twelve months, gradually working through all the personality/life issues. If you are able to complete the whole year in this way you will have drawn closer to the high-energy vibration of the angels. Then, as the following year begins, you will be much more familiar with the angels and can work with the Angel for Every Day programme again in a more intimate way. The more you work with the angels, the closer you will be to their energy, and the greater your rapport with them as, wrapped in their unconditional love, you become more accepting of life's challenges. Work, then, to achieve your aspirations and real life purpose, gradually rewriting the template of your life to find contentment.

Sending Love and Light from
Angela McGerr

A New Year dawns – time for
self-renewal or a change of direction?

Nadiel, angel ruler of Capricorn

Combining my loving golden energy and green rays of living light I bring you strength of bronze to plant your feet firmly on Earth and to give stamina for your personal development. For you have the determination and thoroughness to achieve so much, provided that you do not lose confidence in yourself or your abilities. You have everything to play for in this game of life if you have not become too set in your ways. As this New Year commences, let go of preconceptions and look again to your aspirations. What would you like to achieve? Let those aspirations be built on strong foundations, and be nurtured with true conviction. Learn to take small setbacks in your stride and use your innate ability to face and conquer new challenges. My earth energy brings you the inner strength to reach out towards beauty and fulfilment.

Nadiel's Capricorn, an earth sign, is ruled by Saturn, planet of overcoming challenge to find peace and serenity. Saturn's ruler is the angel Cassiel.

As the year turns, Nadiel and the other chapter angels suggest this is your opportunity for either change or self-renewal. It's time to evaluate your past year and make some decisions – was it all you wished it to be, or were you a little disappointed? Did you face challenges? If the year went well, why not work with the angels to build further confidence and determination to make this year as good or even better? If it was a disappointment, think about making changes in job, house, country or relationships, so that by next December you will look back with a greater sense of fulfilment.

On the opposite page are the qualities and skills addressed in Nadiel's chapter; you may have the right balance in each of them, or perhaps you need a little help? Just at the moment, you may be glad of some angelic support, and if this is the case, read on.

Personal qualities linked with Capricorn and Nadiel:
  Confidence, inner conviction, practicality
  Thoroughness, determination, staying power

Elemental angels offer these earth strengths:
  Inner strength, wisdom and calmness
  Growth and expansion of positive emotions

The ruling planetary angel (Cassiel) influences:
  Ability to embrace change and/or conquer challenge

A simple way to start working on any of these issues is to invoke Nadiel to help you.

First, decide on your priority, and whether you need to bolster personal qualities or interactive skills. Which word or phrase from the list on page 15 best fits your immediate need? Now turn this into an invocation: *"Nadiel, Nadiel, Nadiel, please help me with my (insert the word or phrase you selected, e.g. confidence and inner conviction). In love and light, love and light, love and light."*

If you prefer, you can say *"for my highest good"* instead of *"in love and light"*; you will find this wording is given in some of the chapter invocations. The main thing is to begin with the angel's name three times and to end with your chosen words repeated three times.

When you first make your invocation close your eyes (to focus on what you can feel, rather than see) and hold out your hands in front of you, to try to feel the angel energy come in as a response. Relax your hands and allow yourself to feel.

A response from Nadiel is usually like warmth, a breeze, tingling, tickling or gentle pressure. To begin with it's often felt on the fingers or palms, and more on the left (taking or accepting) hand. When you feel this, thank Nadiel for coming to your aid. If you don't feel very much to start with, keep trying, as it takes a little practice.

Write this first invocation on a post-it note and put it up in your home where you will see it every day, or memorise it. Say your invocation as often as you need to – **the angels are always there.**

You could empower your invocation further by using the colours, flowers or crystals for Nadiel, Cassiel and other Capricorn angels suggested in this chapter.

Do you need first to make time to think about what you need?

Eth, angel of time, says that time is fluid:
I am the angel who rules time, but it is not as you think. Time is fluid, yet endless, as it passes in a stream through my hands, past, present and future. It flows as the symbol of eternity, back and forth and around, sometimes fast and sometimes slower. The idea that time is fixed is only a construct in the mind of mankind. I make the time stream flow, and if for your highest good you need to change the flow, call on me to help you make this happen.

Making time with Eth. Eth can help you to find the time to do these things. This is how to invoke Eth: *"Eth, Eth, Eth, please help me to find the time to think about myself, and focus on what will truly make me happy, if for my highest good. In love and light, love and light, love and light."*

Here are two positive affirmations to try with Nadiel. You can alter them to suit your own needs. If you decide to do one, write it down and place it somewhere where you can say it every day until you feel you are achieving your objective.

To increase determination and inner conviction: *"Nadiel, I know I am capable of the determination, confidence and inner conviction to achieve my aspirations in life. Guided by your love I shall be methodical in pursuing these aims and I shall not give up until I succeed."*

To become more down-to-earth, practical and thorough: *"Nadiel, I have new aspirations but I need to be more practical to really make things happen. With your loving assistance I shall be realistic and thorough in my approach, and I will build the stamina to make my dreams into reality."*

Capricorn colours can add focus if you wear them or bring them into your life in some way while addressing this month's issues.

Using green for personal or inner growth. Earth sign months always include green. This month has emerald for healing the heart. It calms, and helps to build the inner conviction that is needed to succeed. Leaf green is for inner growth and expansion of your positive qualities.

Turquoise-blue and green-bronze for wisdom and staying power. Turquoise is for the wisdom to recognise and take up the right opportunity when it presents itself. Bronze helps with the physical strength, stamina and staying power you may also need.

Capricorn crystals. Crystals in the same colours will help this month, i.e. emerald, malachite, peridot or turquoise. Crystals bring extra energy and can be programmed during the exercises and meditations. Use a peridot, if you have one, for the green colour-breathing exercise on page 23. Cassiel crystals (for the meditation on pages 32–3) are black and white agate, gold sheen or snowflake obsidian or rutilated quartz.

Achaiah, angel of nature's secrets, suggests breathing the green of new leaves to expand attributes such as determination, confidence, conviction or practicality.

If you have a peridot crystal (see page 21) hold this in your left hand to programme while doing this breathing exercise. Imagine that within you, in your heart, you have the potential to light a green flame for growth and expansion. Then invoke the angel:

- *"Achaiah, Achaiah, Achaiah, help me to breathe in the power of green to expand my heart with positive energy so I can send this to my emotions. In love and light, love and light, love and light."*
- Now imagine that you are breathing in green light that flows down into your heart, igniting a green flame within you.
- Continue breathing and feel the flame growing in intensity and radiating throughout your body and energising your positive emotions/attributes. You know what you need this flame to do.
- Feel the power of green expanding your own true potential as well as building the practicality needed to realise this.
- Now, as you breathe out green light, it swirls around you forming an invisible cloak of green, surrounding you with an aura of energy for staying power.
- Cover your left hand (the one with the crystal) with your right hand, asking the angels to seal in the positive energy you have generated. Carry this crystal around to further boost your positive attitude.
- Thank the angels for their help.

New Year – time for new ideas or change of direction? Nadiel is also the angel of moving house, job or even country. Perhaps now is the time to let Nadiel and other angels aid you to make major changes and find your true destiny.

The confidence to move house, job or country. Ask Nadiel to guide you by saying: *"Nadiel, Nadiel, Nadiel, please guide me in my heart on whether or not I should move house (or job or country). In love and light, love and light, love and light."*

For dream guidance on moving or changing direction. Write Nadiel's name on a piece of paper with this invocation and place under your pillow when you go to bed, mentally asking Nadiel to guide you in a lucid dream. Say: *"Nadiel, Nadiel, Nadiel, let my dreams guide me by clarifying what I should be doing next. In love and light, love and light, love and light."*

Staying power and success, if you feel blocked with your move.
Invoke Zadkiel, angel of abundance, wisdom and success, to help by
saying: *"Zadkiel, Zadkiel, Zadkiel, please bring me abundance of success
with moving on in life. In love and light, love and light, love and light."*

Help from Oriel, angel of destiny. If in doubt, ask Oriel whether
moving will help you to follow your true destiny: *"Oriel, Oriel,
Oriel, I ask for your guidance on how and where to find my true destiny.
In love and light, love and light, love and light."* Oriel often works with
Tabris, angel of free will (see page 30).

To add physical strength/stamina to your determination. Call on
Zeruch, angel of strength by saying: *"Zeruch, Zeruch, Zeruch, please
bring me your strength and stamina to physically sustain me until I
complete my aims. In love and light, love and light, love and light."*

Capricorn is an earth sign. Use Mother Earth's positive energy in different ways to help your own feeling of renewal.

For energy balance, Achaiah, angel of nature's secrets, suggests some essential oils to help heal, balance and energise energy centres involved in this month's issues. Use an oil burner or float two or three drops of oil on a small amount of water to fragrance a room while doing any of the exercises in this Capricorn month. Or you could place a drop or two on your pulse points inside the wrists. The relevant four chakra energy centres are: base (foundations, practicality, grounding); solar (positive emotions and stamina); heart (calmness, conviction, inner expansion); throat (opportunity and truth). (See also Scorpio page 267.) NB: Always take great care with oils if pregnant.

- **(Base) base of spine:** Patchouli for strengthening/grounding
- **(Solar) solar plexus:** Vetivert for protecting/balancing energy
- **(Heart) heart region:** Rose for healing, opening, expanding heart
- **(Throat) throat area:** Camomile to aid the communication of truth

Special plants for Nadiel and Capricorn. Pansies, amaranthus and comfrey are special Capricorn flowers. Use these and/or pine, or pine cones, and willow twigs to make an arrangement to remind you about earth energy this month and how to tap into it with angels.

Zuphlas, guardian angel of trees, who features on the next page, suggests pine essential oil for cleansing and invigorating, especially when used in a bath. Also juniper, to counteract negativity in a room, and cedarwood, to strengthen your connection to the angels.

Can't see the wood for the trees? Zuphlas offers a special message and exercise on page 29 to help you to be more relaxed by getting closer to earth/tree magic. Invoke Zuphlas by saying: *"Zuphlas, Zuphlas, Zuphlas, please help me to relax and have patience enough to see beyond immediate issues. Like your trees I need to take a long-term view of what to do, and I ask for your support with this, for my highest good, highest good, highest good."*

Nature helps you to de-stress and renew strength in this earth sign month in order to consider what to do in your year ahead.

Zuphlas, angel of trees, gives you his message:
On gentle zephyrs of wind you may sense me gliding to Mother Earth filling leaves, bark and branches of my trees with loving energy and balance. When you give care and attention to trees you embrace me also and I return this love to you; this is a long-term philosophy. Take a little time out to renew your connection to Mother Earth and nature, and to be healed with the pure strength and ancient sacred wisdom of my trees.

If life is stressful just now, Zuphlas gives this advice:
Try to spend even a little time in the open air, for even in winter nature is merely asleep and waiting to awaken. Find somewhere to sit among trees. Read my message, then close your eyes and allow the strong yet gentle energy of the trees to flow into you, bringing a sense of relaxation, connection to nature and perfect balance.

If you just know that this year you want to change your life completely and need more determination:

A message from Tabris:
I beckon to you from the Door to Light, out of which my golden radiance shines. I seek to guide your footsteps, for many are the doors that open during your life, but few will be your Doors to Light.

Bringing choices forward: Write the name of Tabris on a post-it note, put it up where you will see it every morning. Say: "*Tabris, Tabris, Tabris, I am looking for the Door to Light in my life. Please guide me towards the opportunity to find this Door leading to a happier and more fulfilling future. In love and light, love and light, love and light.*" Be a little patient.

If you need to decide between two options. Say: "*Tabris, Tabris, Tabris, I now have a decision to make and I want this to be for my highest good. Please guide my steps to my personal Door to Light. In love and light, love and light, love and light.*" Say this as often as you need to until you have made a decision that feels right in your heart.

Capricorn is ruled by Saturn, the planet of challenge. Sometimes we have to face and conquer challenges and try to emerge with serenity. If you have such a situation in your life you could try this meditation with Cassiel.

➤ Sit quietly and close your eyes; place the challenge you face in your heart.

➤ If you have a Cassiel crystal (see page 21) hold this in your left hand.

➤ Invoke Cassiel by saying: "*Cassiel, Cassiel, Cassiel, please be with me to help me face and conquer this challenge, so that I can look forward to the year ahead. In love and light, love and light, love and light.*"

➤ Breathe as deeply as possible, imagining you are breathing in pure, white energy, right down through your body, even into your toes.

➤ With each out-breath you are letting go of negative feelings, such as fear or worry about what you are facing – until you have let all this go.

- With the next breath send this light through your toes and down to the heart of Mother Earth, until it connects with the crystal at her heart.
- Now breathe this crystalline energy back through your toes and draw it up to your heart.
- As your heart is bathed in sparkling crystalline light it helps you to intuit how to overcome your challenge.
- Send light up through the top of your head, to illuminate your mind to decide what to do, so the outcome will return you to peace and serenity.
- Ask Cassiel to help you seal in your positive feelings, and also to complete the programming of your crystal. Thank him for his help.
- Keep the crystal with you for confidence until your challenge is resolved.

Angels, the elements and courage

"Returning recently from the first weekend of Angela's Melchisadec Mystery School, I arrived late at night at the airport to find Geneva covered in ice and snow and with a temperature of −5° C.

"The airport had been closed the day before for nine hours. With this news on landing I followed everybody else into a huge queue for a taxi. While standing there in the cold I suddenly felt impelled to drive my car instead, which was parked in the underground garage at the airport. I felt excited by this daring idea, since I am normally very scared of driving in icy conditions.

"I asked for angelic protection and, with this new feeling of strength in me, I drove the car home. The traffic was extremely slow and the cars were dangerously close together. I passed three public buses that unloaded their passengers and refused to carry on driving. My heart was pumping but I just had to carry on. Finally I turned into the icy driveway of our home, skidding slightly, but I had made it home safe and sound. My hands were trembling, my heart just bouncing everywhere, but I felt exhilarated to have stood up to this challenge; I just felt great. I thanked my angel. Only later did I learn from my family that I had been driving on summer tyres …"

(from Dagmar Walker, Switzerland)

Abundance of help from Zadkiel

Katalyn approached me to ask how to call on angels for abundance of help in combating her nervousness prior to a job interview and I suggested she invoke Zadkiel, angel of abundance, wisdom and success. For the invocation I sent her, see page 54.

This was her reply:
"Recently, I had an interview for a job and I was worried because I was very nervous. A friend of mine gave me a piece of lapis lazuli to hold and I held it tightly on my way to the interview, also repeating the Zadkiel invocation you gave me. When I was inside the building I had to wait about 15 minutes and I was so nervous that I kept repeating your words. A few minutes before I was called, I suddenly had the feeling that somebody was putting a warm blanket over my body and I was not nervous anymore. The stone in my hand was also warm. I really had the feeling that there was somebody or something with me. It was a nice feeling travelling all over my body – even my heart was warm. I had the feeling that I could move mountains."

(from Katalyn Feijens, Belgium)

Listen intuitively to your heart to find the right focus for life or work.

Cambiel, angel ruler of Aquarius

Like the Water Carrier of my sign, I bring the silver-blue water of life to heal the grail of your heart, and to allow your inner feelings to grow and develop to their full potential. For above all I urge you to listen to your own intuition, and to follow your heart at this time. As the white fire of lightning may flash in the sky, the power of air and fire manifests through me to light the amber spark of your visionary aspirations. In this, my time of the year, find the right focus in life and work to maintain your vision, asking my aid if you have been hurt by life. I urge you to be true to yourself and your ideals in the rightness of your words and actions. Continue to empathise with others, for in today's difficult world your skills are truly beyond price.

Cambiel's Aquarius, an air sign, is ruled by Uranus, planet of creativity and transformation. Uranus is ruled by Uriel.

It is still early in the year; but time can pass you by. If you are focusing on change or transformation, Cambiel counsels you to listen to your own inner self and follow your intuition with regard to your true aspirations and heart's desire. Uriel offers to open your centre of creativity to let these emerge. Other angels inspire and support you with this chance to find a new focus, one that accords with your personal principles and ideals, bolsters your own self-belief and in some way, benefits others as well.

The qualities and skills opposite are addressed in Cambiel's chapter; you may have the right balance in each of them, or do you need a little help with one? If so, then this chapter will help you.

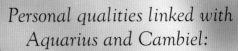

*Personal qualities linked with
Aquarius and Cambiel:*
Identification of true
aspirations/ambitions
Principles, ideals, integrity, empathy

*Elemental angels offer these
air strengths:*
Visionary inspiration and intuition
Flower/essential-oil energy healing

*The ruling planetary angel
(Uriel) influences:*
Creative energy for self-
transformation or a fresh start
Cleansing, purifying, revitalising sacral area

A simple way to get started with Cambiel on one of these issues is to invoke Cambiel to help you.

First, decide on your priority. Now select one of the words or phrases on page 39 that meets one of your needs. Now turn this into an invocation as follows: *"Cambiel, Cambiel, Cambiel, please help me with my (insert the words you selected, e.g. true aspirations). In love and light, love and light, love and light."*

When you first make your invocation close your eyes (vision is the strongest of the senses) and hold out your hands in front of you, to try to feel the response of Cambiel to your request.

If you continue to do your invocation (or make invocations to other angels as well), your connection becomes stronger and you will gradually feel more angelic energy.

Each angel will give you a slightly different response, so you will know which one is which.

Do keep practising – the more you do it the easier it becomes. Remember also to thank your angel for coming.

You could also add an affirmation, for positive focus. See page 44 for some suggestions or make up your own version. Again, keep making your affirmation as often as you can (say, every day) until you feel things starting to change.

As Aquarius is an air sign, Zikiel, angel of comets and meteors, offers you a visionary flash of inspiration from the sky.

Zikiel's message:

I guide the comets and meteorites in their eternal passage through space, telling of man's galactic origins. A swirl of bright cosmic dust shows my passing, but as I pass I can bring you the sudden brilliant inspiration that you might need to make a quantum leap in life. Programme a crystal with my name and keep it with you until you receive your insight. Ask me also to guide your heart, so you will know the insight is right for you.

Programme an inspiration crystal. Choose a clear quartz crystal and hold it in your left hand. Read Zikiel's message over this crystal and then hold it in both hands, mentally asking Zikiel to help you to breathe heart energy into your crystal to seal in your programming with love. Keep it in a pocket or bag, or under your pillow, until you feel you have gained your insight. If it feels right in your heart then act upon it.

Try one of these two positive affirmations with Cambiel.

For the intuitive vision to find new aspirations: *"Cambiel, I need to re-kindle my aspirations and with your support I will clarify my vision of where I wish to go in life. Thank you for helping me to understand that within me is the intuitive ability to find vision and focus, so that filled with hope I may once again move forward."*

Maintaining integrity with ideals and principles: *"Cambiel, I turn away from compromise in order to stand by my principles. With your loving support I will find the strength and balance to build my self-confidence, and I shall continue to pursue my personal truth with rightness and integrity."*

Colours in this chapter are for ambition, intuition, creativity and empathy – use them to aid with these Aquarius issues.

Wearing or using Aquarius colours. Wearing the appropriate colours reminds you what you want to achieve with the angels of this month. Aquarius colours are sea green/aqua, blue, silver and amber.

Amber kindles creativity to innovate/transform self or situations.

Silver develops your intuition. Silver (moon energy with Gabriel) is for intuition as well as balancing energies and opening the heart towards others in order to build more empathy and understanding.

Blue and blue-green are for wisdom, empathy in communication and calmness. There are more angelic blue colours than any other shade. Aquarius has deep blue for wisdom on how to maintain principles and ideals, and sky blue to increase the effectiveness of your communications with others, as well as being truthful with self. Also blue-green, which heals and calms emotional issues that may be blocking your progress in life.

If you want to develop your powers of intuition, think silver. Try breathing silver energy with Gabriel, angel of the moon. If you can do this exercise in moonlight this maximises the energy; a full moon is best of all.

➤ Close your eyes and begin taking deep breaths of pure, white energy, breathing out any negative emotions, until you start to feel relaxed.

➤ Then invoke Gabriel like this: *"Gabriel, Gabriel, Gabriel, help me to breathe the power of silver into my open heart to develop and guide my intuition. In love and light, love and light, love and light."*

➤ Imagine that you are able to breathe in a silver energy spiral, which comes up clockwise from Mother Earth.

➤ The silver energy ray flows in through the base of your spine and as it passes through your heart it fills it with silver to correct your feminine (intuitive) energy balance.

➤ As you continue breathing silver it spirals up from your heart and through the crown of your head.

➤ Send it on to the moon to anchor your source of intuition and maintain the connection, remembering to thank the angels for their help.

➤ Do this exercise as often as you need to further develop your intuitive skills.

Aquarius is an air sign; nature's tools to aid focus on inspiration.

A message from Achaiah, angel of nature's secrets:
I am the angel of nature's grace – privy to her secrets of colour, fragrance and form. Mine is the beauty of butterfly and bee in sun-filled meadow, the delicate and pleasing petals of a flower, the spiral symmetry of a shell. In this air sign month I ask you to remember that without air neither mankind nor flower nor butterfly will grow.

Plants, trees and flowers for Cambiel and Aquarius. All kinds of fruits and fruit trees are connected with this sign, including apple, pear and elderberry. Special Aquarius flowers are orchids but all blue or blue-green flowers are good. Arrange some of these to remind you to call the angels or make any chosen affirmations about this month's issues and call on Achaiah to inspire you by saying: *"Achaiah, Achaiah, Achaiah, with the beauty of your flowers help me to focus on the visionary inspiration I need in life, for my highest good. In love and light, love and light, love and light."*

Oils and essences. As Aquarius is an air sign, why not gain extra energy by scenting a room with appropriate fragrances, especially when doing an exercise in this chapter? Use oils from the orchids, fruits or trees mentioned opposite, or rose and jasmine are always excellent as they are close to the angelic vibration and summon all angels to help you. Float two or three drops of oil on a small bowl of water, or use on pulse points.

Feathers and air. Feathers are linked with angels and also represent the Air element. White feathers are a sign from the angels that you should be looking for ways to find inner peace. Look out for tiny white feathers inside or outside, and collect any you find. Keep them to help you think about angels. You can also place or stick them around a small mirror to enhance their air and inspirational energy. See also the true life stories on pages 83, 226, 227.

Arad, a silver angel to bolster your self-belief, ideals and principles.

Arad, guardian angel of beliefs, has this message for you:
Do you need reassurance about what you believe yourself to be? Ask me to send my powerful silver energy to fill your soul, for this is the individual, essential core of you which makes you the person you really are and gives rise to your personality. If your self-belief is being tested, call on me to aid you. I fill your heart with the power of unconditional love to guard your very self and help maintain the purity of your principles and ideals.

To call on Arad for help: *"Arad, Arad, Arad, I ask for you to be with me to support my self-belief so that I can stand against those who undermine me. With your love I can be faithful to my ideals, living my life in accordance with my personal principles. In love and light, love and light, love and light."*

Rikbiel, a golden angel to find empathy with others, especially with relationships.

Rikbiel, angel of the power of love, says:
I drive the Light Chariot of the Creator, fashioned from dazzling golden sun rays, which travels at the speed of Love to resolve and heal all problems, for whatever or wherever they may be, be assured that Love will find the way.

To invoke Rikbiel, say: *"Rikbiel, Rikbiel, Rikbiel, I ask for your guidance, for I know that with this pure, positive energy, though it may take a little time, with the power of love all things are possible. I understand that problems can be resolved. In love and light, love and light, love and light."*

When using this invocation, do be patient, for perhaps things need to be set into motion. The angels ask you to remember that it is not a magic-wand situation – problem-solving can take a little time.

Although an Air sign, Aquarius is the carrier of water from the pool of life. If you channel this into your heart it opens the flower of heart's desire.

If you want to follow your heart, Pagiel, angel of the heart's desire, says:
My loving energy flows around you in a bright stream. Allow this stream to carry you forwards, at your own pace with surrender and trust, as it conveys you gradually ever nearer towards your ambition. With my aid the water of life flows into the chalice of your heart, and when the flower of your heart opens, in the centre of this flower I enable you to perceive your true heart's desire.

Invoking Pagiel: *"Pagiel, Pagiel, Pagiel, let your energy support me and maintain my focus in life as I decide on the first steps towards my goal, of following my heart's desire. In love and light, love and light, love and light."*

Heart's desire? Pagiel says that you must recheck from time to time that it truly is your heart's desire upon which you are focusing your energy.

Angelic help to focus on ambitions and aspirations.

To ask for success in an interview. Are you due to attend an interview that you think leads to achieving your ambitions? Invoke Zadkiel to bring you success by saying (before you go in): *"Zadkiel, Zadkiel, Zadkiel, please be with me to bring me success if it's for my highest good, highest good, highest good."* A Zadkiel crystal (turquoise or lapis lazuli) in your pocket/bag also aids focus. If you are not successful with it maybe it was not for your highest good. See also the true life story on page 35.

Need to lighten up a little? Call on Tagas, angel of music.
Tagas says:
I sound the silver chord that comes from the void to resonate with your soul in the melodies of life. My silver wings trail music from the stars themselves to teach you the power of musical harmony and to enrich your world with song. Take a moment to sing out loud for sheer joy of being alive. Singing for a few minutes (even to yourself) is excellent therapy.

Unable to focus because your life is chaotic? Sadriel, angel of order, helps to bring your day, home or life back into order. Say: *"Sadriel, Sadriel, Sadriel, I cannot see what to do unless the chaos of my life is brought into order; please help me. In love and light, love and light, love and light."*

Eth, angel of time, bends time on your behalf. Sadriel often works together with Eth. Invoke Eth to help also: *"Eth, Eth, Eth, I ask for your help to bend time for something really important today, and I pledge to organise my life better in future, for my highest good. In love and light, love and light, love and light."*

For special creative and innovative energy. Wear something orange (this is the colour of creativity, innovation and transformation) and ask Uriel, angel of fire and amber, to boost your energy. You could wear a piece of amber (Uriel's stone containing fire of a thousand suns) or better still, do the meditation on the following pages.

Aquarius is ruled by Uranus, the planet of transformation and creativity.

This is a wonderful opportunity for you to work with Uriel, ruler of Uranus. Uriel says:
Many and mysterious are the ways I manifest on Mother Earth. I descend in dazzling lightning bringing my mysterious alchemical fire that cleanses and purifies, before I offer the power of recharging your centre of creativity, innovation and transformation.

- Sit quietly and close your eyes.
- If you have a piece of amber (Uriel's special stone, optional), hold this in your left hand.
- Start taking deep breaths in and imagine that you are breathing in the power of amber (the orange-yellow fire of a thousand suns).
- As you breathe in say in your head: *"I breathe in the power of orange and amber."*
- Breathe these breaths down to your sacral area (behind navel).
- Mentally ask Uriel to help you completely cleanse and purify this area.

~ Then replenish by making one or all of these affirmations, as appropriate:

"With this power I am transformed in mind and body."

"With this power I ignite my creative energy."

"With this power I allow my true aspirations to emerge."

~ Thank Uriel for his assistance and ask him to seal in your affirmation with love and light, plus seal the programming into your crystal if you had one.

~ Keep the crystal with you until you feel you no longer need it.

Travelling through life with the angels

"I have travelled for many years alone throughout the world as a single woman, but never have I felt truly alone. I have been to many wild, strange, crazy and at times scary parts of the world, but always the angels have been there by my side guiding me forward. I have learnt through all the different experiences I have had to trust and follow my intuition and the guidance of the angels completely, even in situations where everything seems hazy and uncertain and I just don't know what direction my life will take me in next. I know if I fully trust that everything will work out for my highest good it will, and it always has.

"I have been on wild boat trips in Laos, insane bus trips through the Andes, floated down the Ganges in the middle of the night on a simple wooden boat. I've soaked myself in steaming hot mud pools in Iceland, climbed active volcanoes in Nicaragua, hiked in the wilds of Alaska and visited lost cities in Colombia – always with the angels. In every single situation they have been there by my side, laughing with me through the fun times and supporting and comforting me in the uncertain times, and never has their love and support not been a part of my life.

"My daily ritual, wherever I am, is to invoke the angels to be in my life and to visualise myself being surrounded by Michael's cloak of protection. Many times when I have been walking alone, especially at night, I have actually felt Michael's presence by my side walking with me forward into the light. Other people have seen me walking with what they assume is a friend, so it doesn't appear that I am alone. At times I feel people just sense that I am well protected and that Michael's cobalt-blue cloak is protecting me from any possible danger.

"I have found that the angels' support and love is more comforting than that of other people around me as they are always there, regardless of the time of day, the location or the circumstances. They always understand and are ready and waiting to lend a helping hand. I have truly experienced that the more I trust and am open to the angels being a part of my life, the more amazing and incredible things manifest into my life."

(from Alison Joy Kyle, Sydney, Australia)

Time to be more discerning in your passions or commitments.

Barakiel, angel ruler of Pisces

I offer you the gentle silver protection of my loving energy. Your intelligence and thoughtfulness are qualities that others admire; I enfold you with my love to shield your sensitivity for you are both passionate and compassionate, often giving your all to people and causes. You are capable of remarkable creativity, but take care in the causes you espouse, for you will achieve more by showing greater discernment. When you are approached in these matters take the time to consider from your heart whether or not they are right for you. To your deep imagination call on my assistance to enhance psychic and intuitive skills before making a commitment you may later regret. Seek blue-green energy of water to soothe your emotions and temperament when necessary and to bring you gently back to balance and harmony.

Barakiel's Pisces, a water sign, is ruled by Neptune, planet of healing the heart and emotions. Neptune's ruler is Phuel.

Barakiel and the angels of this chapter say this is a time you can use to review all that you do, identifying the people and causes genuinely worthy of your commitment, especially if you have made mistakes in the past. You are gifted in many ways, but they urge you not to let others take advantage, for there is only so much you can do with your time. Use your sensitivity to be perceptive when faced with certain choices. Then with the help of Phuel, be calm, balanced and discerning with your decisions, for you are capable of great achievement.

Opposite you will find the qualities addressed by the angels in this chapter, to help you review how your life is progressing at this point in the year. See if these include attributes you need help with, and if so, it is worthwhile reading and absorbing this chapter.

Personal qualities linked with Pisces and Barakiel:

Sensitivity, thoughtfulness, discernment
Creative imagination and inspiration

Elemental angels offer these water strengths:

Calmness and clarity when considering commitment
Magic of nature for psychic perception/development

The ruling planetary angel (Phuel) influences:

Soothing and healing any emotional
turbulence/excess

A simple way to get started with Barakiel on one of these issues.

First, decide whether you need some support with one of the attributes in this chapter, summarised on page 63. Do you have too much or too little of one of them? If so, the angels help you bring your personal qualities into balance. Select something you need from the qualities list. Now turn this into an invocation as follows: *"Barakiel, Barakiel, Barakiel, please help me with my (insert the word you selected, e.g. sensitivity). In love and light, love and light, love and light."*

When you first make your invocation close your eyes (to focus on what you can feel rather than see) and hold out your hands in front of you, palms up, to try to feel the angel energy come in as a response.

Don't worry if you find this difficult at first. Try to relax your hands and wait a few moments after you make the invocation. Let yourself gently feel. It may be a gentle or soft pressure on your palms, or a sort of tickling, or it could be something slightly different like a flash of light in your inner vision – you are not imagining it.

If you continue to do your invocation (or make invocations to other angels as well), your connection becomes stronger and you will gradually feel more and more angelic energy.

This exercise is only a means of training. Gradually you will find that you only need to say the angel's name once (even mentally) to feel the energy coming in to you.

Always thank the angels.

Pisces is a water sign. Haurvatat, guardian angel of rivers, offers a moment of calmness and clarity to evaluate a situation.

Haurvatat's personal message:

The river of life is mysterious; sometimes it is very swift, with strong currents that carry you too fast into things, but sometimes I can bring a point of stillness when it hardly moves, and all is laid before you in startling clarity. Take this time with me for the course of your own river to be revealed.

To invoke Haurvatat say: *"Haurvatat, Haurvatat, Haurvatat, please be with me in the flow in my life and guide me to a place of stillness to see what to do next. In love and light, love and light, love and light."*

If you can sit by a river, stream or brook while saying the invocation, you could connect directly to Haurvatat's energy. Write Haurvatat's message down and read it out loud while listening to the sound of water flowing. Then do the invocation. Close your eyes and see what your heart feels you should do.

Try one of these three positive affirmations with Barakiel.

For showing greater discernment: *"Barakiel, thank you for my sensitivity that gives me great understanding and sympathy for others. With your support and protection I build emotional strength and ask you to help me to show greater discernment and intuition over people and causes."*

If you need more grounding: *"Barakiel, with your loving support and strength I bring myself back down to earth for grounding and manifesting my next steps. Let my strong intuitive skills be balanced by power of decision and action, for my highest good."*

For latent artistic skills: *"Barakiel, I deserve a chance to allow the artistic imagination that I know I have within me to be expressed. I will bring forth this talent for now is the time for me to create something beautiful that will bring joy to myself as well as others."*

These are the colours for thoughtfulness, calmness, imagination and psychic/spiritual development.

The Pisces colours of indigo blue, blue-green, mauve-violet and purple help in a variety of ways. Wearing these colours can help you to focus on Pisces issues. Pisces is ruled by Neptune, whose ruler is Phuel, lord of all the waters. This includes tides of earth and powers of moon – remember these affect your moods.

Restful blues aid calmness of thought. If you have trouble resting or finding calmness for thinking, indigo blue will help you. Mid-blue aids with saying the right thing at the right time, especially if a commitment is involved. Blue-green soothes and heals sensitive or emotional situations.

Spiritual violet is for imagination and psychic development. Mauve-violet is a colour to wear for spirituality and when it deepens to purple, for magic and psychic skills/development. But remember not all psychic skills are spiritually linked, so ensure you ask the angels to guide you here (see also the exercise on pages 70–1).

Breathing violet with Aratron, angel of magic, for healing the third eye/brow area and reaching out towards nature's magic to find a psychic skill that is right for you.

Close your eyes and begin taking deep breaths of pure, white energy, breathing out any negative emotions, until you start to feel relaxed. Then invoke Aratron in this way:

➤ *"Aratron, Aratron, Aratron, I ask you to bring me the violet ray of angelic magic and transmutation. In love and light, love and light, love and light."*
➤ Now imagine that you can breathe in this light and with every breath it is going deeper into you, until it reaches and fills your heart.
➤ When you feel your heart has absorbed the violet energy, send it towards your forehead (third eye chakra), the psychic energy centre of the body.

- As you do this mentally make this colour affirmation:

"Aratron, with power of violet I transmute all illusions from within me and replenish my inner self. Protected by your love I reach out to retrieve the magic of nature that is my ancient wisdom. Help me to access and develop this with the right teacher, if for my highest good."

- Pause for guidance from Aratron in the form of tingling, warmth or a message of some kind in your heart.

- Breathe the violet energy out, gradually forming wings of light around you.

- Thank Aratron for his help and wait for further guidance/synchronicity.

Further guidance from Aratron might indicate the ability to use earth magic involving crystals, metals, oils, flowers, etc., energy healing of some kind, shamanic wisdom or another ancient skill to benefit self and others.

Nature angels and water soothe sensitive emotions.

Sachluph, angel of plants, says:
I glow with the beauty and healing that plants bring to mankind. Water of life causes my plants to grow and flourish in deserts, mountains and jungles. Like my plants, you, too, need water of life.

Water plants and blue or mauve flowers for Barakiel and Pisces.
Trees growing near water, like willows, are connected with this sign, as are water plants like water lily (lotus), iris, ferns and all types of rushes. An arrangement of these can remind you to call on the angels of this month, or you could float a suitable flower in a shallow bowl when doing meditations or exercises during this month.

Water features for emotional calmness. As Pisces is a water sign, why not use water in some way? You might consider an indoor water feature, which when plugged in will allow you to hear the gentle sound of water in your home and would certainly help with the invocations opposite.

Protection from sensitivity and healing past hurts.

Are you recovering from a broken heart? Mupiel is the angel who mends hearts. Sit quietly and take some really deep breaths. Invoke Mupiel by saying: *"Mupiel, Mupiel, Mupiel, please bring me the cool blue-green of water to flow in and heal my heart so that it will open once more to love, for my highest good, highest good, highest good."* Try to really feel the power of water soothing and healing your heart, so that it can reopen to new love. You could also do the meditation with Phuel in this chapter, on pages 80–1.

Blue heals and protects your sensitivity. Michael, ruler of Wednesday, protects you and brings cobalt blue for emotional strength when you need it. Invoke Michael at any time by saying: *"Michael, Michael, Michael, please be with me to bring strength and protection. In love and light, love and light, love and light."* See also the meditation on pages 152–3. Michael also helps you find your personal truth.

Beauty of plants and nature aid creative imagination.

Invoking Sachluph to help generally with creative expression.
Sachluph, angel of plants, may be able to artistically inspire you.
Hold a Pisces plant (see page 72). Say: *"Sachluph, Sachluph, Sachluph,
please show me how the beauty, fragrance and form of your plants can
inspire my imagination and infuse my soul with inspiration, allowing my
own abilities to manifest. In love and light, love and light, love and light."*

To add to the energy of making this invocation you could use an
oil or essence of one of the flowers for Pisces (or rose and jasmine,
which summon all angels). Scent the room while working at home
on Pisces issues, or while doing a special invocation, exercise or
meditation in this chapter.

After saying this invocation close your eyes and allow your intuition
to come to the fore, as true inspiration comes from heart and soul.

For different types of creative inspiration.

Radueriel, angel of artistic inspiration (usually visual arts), can help you to manifest your inspirational thoughts. Say: *"Radueriel, Radueriel, Radueriel, give me (or I have received) the creative inspiration I need to further my work, please help me to express it in the appropriate medium to help as many people as possible. In love and light, love and light, love and light."*

If it is poetry or literature you are writing: Use the same invocation, but instead of Radueriel, substitute the name of Israfel three times (he is angel of poetry).

If you are a musician: Again, use the same invocation but substitute the name of Tagas, who is angel of music, to guide you to produce music from your soul, which will speak to the souls of others.

Using the colour violet with the angel Melchisadec to counteract extremes of emotion.

If you could see inside yourself, extreme negative emotions such as fear, sorrow, anger or frustration would appear as dark patches of energy. The colour violet is called the spiritual antiseptic and it can be used to transmute these dark patches back into white light. If you ask Melchisadec from your heart, he brings you an invisible (but very effective) bowl of violet flames.

- To use this amazing energy say: *"Melchisadec, Melchisadec, Melchisadec, please give me a bowl of the violet fire of transmutation. In love and light, love and light, love and light."*
- Visualise an imaginary bowl beside you, filled with dancing violet fire.
- Take a deep breath and breathe into your cupped hands whatever it is that you want to transmute.
- Imagine that you are holding this dark energy within your cupped hands.
- Throw it into the invisible bowl. The violet immediately transmutes the dark energy so that it disappears.

Angels to help you with discernment in dealings with others.

Knowing when to speak out. Michael, ruler of Mercury, is the angel of strength, protection and truth and aids with communication. Invoke Michael like this: *"Michael, Michael, Michael, please bring your loving support to help me deal with this issue, to formulate the words I need, and to find the right moment to say them for the highest good of all concerned. In love and light, love and light, love and light."*

A moment of serenity and thinking time. If everything is a hassle and you just can't focus on what to do, you may benefit from a quiet moment of serenity. Cassiel is ruler of Saturn, the planet of challenge, showing us life is always full of ups and downs. Say: *"Cassiel, Cassiel, Cassiel, please be with me to bring a moment's peace, harmony and serenity. In love and light, love and light, love and light."* Let Cassiel's calm energy soothe your mind.

Kadmiel, a golden angel to help you make balanced commitment decisions.

If you are too imaginative. Imagination, artistic and creative skills are all silver qualities; they are great qualities to have but sometimes they are accompanied by an inability to be down to earth, to focus on day-to-day issues or make some necessary decisions/commitments. If this is you, you may need more gold to balance your silver, as daily life must go on.

Balanced decision-making. If you are putting off a decision (or action) about a commitment, one of the golden angels of good fortune, Kadmiel, says: *You may invoke my loving assistance by using my name to ground, balance your energies and protect yourself. My glowing energy flows around and through you, sent by love.*

If you need this just now, write Kadmiel's name down and keep it in a bag or pocket until you feel you have been supported with golden energy to weigh the issues and make the right decision.

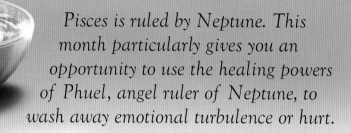

Pisces is ruled by Neptune. This month particularly gives you an opportunity to use the healing powers of Phuel, angel ruler of Neptune, to wash away emotional turbulence or hurt.

- You could do this exercise while in the bath, or swimming, or if this is impossible just use your imagination.
- Sit quietly and focus your attention within, thinking about your desire to calm your emotions. Say Phuel's name three times.
- If you have an aquamarine (one of Phuel's crystals), hold this in your left hand and it will be programmed with healing during this exercise.
- Start taking deep breaths of blue-green energy, breathing them right down through your body.
- Imagine you are walking in a beautiful place of nature.
- Presently you come to a pool of crystal-clear water, reflecting a blue sky.
- Know that with the power of water energy your spirit can go down into this water to be healed and washed clean of emotional turbulence.

- Imagine that you can step into the water and float in it.
- If you wish to you can merge for a short time with the water itself, becoming the medium that nourishes fish and all other water creatures.
- The water is very still, silken in texture and peaceful.
- The sun shines into its depths, lighting the grains of sand at the bottom.
- Let go of your cares; they are washed away by the healing power of water.
- When you feel relaxed, come out of the water (real or imaginary).
- Ask Phuel to seal in your emotional healing, and seal your programmed crystal with silver rays and thank him for his assistance.

Power of water energy

"While doing a course group meditation with the angel Melchisadec during Angela's Mystery School course I was visualising going into an amethyst crystal sphere. My hands were held out, palms up, either side of me (this is the receiving position in meditation) and I was experiencing wonderful rainbow colours in the third eye chakra. Suddenly, a tremendous feeling of calm and wellbeing washing over me in waves of varying colours, starting from reds and purples and then becoming cooler colours of greens and blues – these last two were almost like a shower. When I came out of the meditation, I looked at the palms of my outstretched hands and both palms had water in them ... It really was there; everyone on the course saw it.

"I now realise that water is for healing emotions and in particular the heart. This is what I have to focus on first, before my work as a healer continues. Since the course, a lot of things have happened to do with water, from a hosepipe going out of control and soaking me, glasses of water being knocked off tables, a leaflet being pushed through my door about Magnetic water devices and an invitation to a crop circle talk on, guess what? Water energy patterns in crop-circle glyphs. I think the angels are telling me that my healing work will be helping to heal people's emotions with the power of water."

(from Jackie Wheatley, Egyptian Reiki healer, London)

A larger-than-life sign of an angelic presence

"When I read in Angela's book, A Harmony of Angels, about white feathers being a sign from the angels, I immediately began to receive white feathers. The sceptical part of my brain kept telling me, 'It is a coincidence and you are actively seeking them out to verify that the angels are trying to contact you.' I was unable to sleep and woke up around 2 a.m. every morning, so I became tired and depressed. I began to wonder why I was here, what purpose my life held, and even whether it was all worth the battle of another day. I began praying, as I knew I was at a crossroads in many areas of my life.

"One morning as I walked to work I looked up at the beautiful coloured sky, transfixed by the hues of light. I said, 'Please, give me another sign that you are with me.' At that moment, a lorry turned in to the road. As it came past me I saw on its side a black circle and a white feather about the same size as me (over 5 feet high)!

"I just couldn't believe my eyes! I felt such a surge of joy and warmth that I started to laugh, looked up and said, 'Thank you, thank you, thank you.' I felt the angels were saying to me, 'Well, if this doesn't convince you, nothing will.' I can't argue with that. My self-healing journey with the angels has continued ever since."

(from Michelle Esclapez, London)

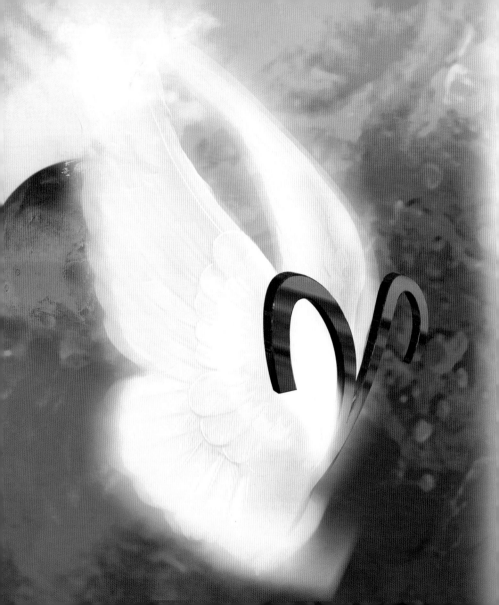

Setting beneficial life goals based on your true needs and wants.

Machidiel, angel ruler of Aries

Mine is the sign that helps you to stand in your personal power, with self-confidence and enthusiasm for life. My energy guides your heart in decision-making, to influence your goals, but be careful. For you may feel you completely understand your heart's desire, but it may be your head's desire and will really not gladden your heart at all. Take this time of my influence during your year to reflect and to consider your real wants and needs rather than the perceived ones you may have held until now. Let me assist you to redefine your goals and to amplify your strengths, so that all the power and passion of your enthusiasm and energy, boosted by my fire colours of red, orange and gold, go into achieving long-term benefits by accomplishing your true purpose in life.

Aries, a fire sign, is ruled by Mars, planet of courage and empowerment. Mars is ruled by Camael.

Machidiel and other angels suggest that you have the ability to do almost anything if you try. However, if your heart is inclined to rule your head, you may have spent a great deal of energy and enthusiasm trying to attain the wrong goals, ones that would not really have made you happy in the long term. Camael brings courage to be yourself and together with other chapter angels, helps you to define more appropriate aims. They offer empowerment with confidence to apply your manifold strengths towards these new aims.

On the opposite page, personal qualities are listed that could be relevant to your current thoughts. You may have these in abundance, but if you need any assistance, the angels are always around to bring loving support.

*Personal qualities linked with
Aries and Machidiel:*
Assertiveness, enthusiasm, awareness
Confidence for individuality and
originality

Elemental angels offer these fire strengths:
Passion for love and/or life itself
Decisiveness in aims, rightness of actions
Letting go of anger

The ruling planetary angel (Camael) influences:
Courage and empowerment to achieve your goals

A simple way to get started on one of these issues is to invoke Machidiel to help you.

Look at the list of attributes or personal qualities featured in this chapter (see page 87). Do you need any help with one or more of them? If so, decide which is your priority. Machidiel and various other angels in the chapter will offer you support to address this issue. Choose one of the words that meets your need, and turn this into an invocation as follows: *"Machidiel, Machidiel, Machidiel, please help me with my (insert the word you selected, e.g. assertiveness). In love and light, love and light, love and light."*

When you first make your invocation close your eyes (to focus on what you can feel rather than see) and hold out your hands in front of you (palms up is good) to try to feel the angel's response.

You may feel a lot or just a little tingling, warmth, a cool breeze or pressure around your fingers, particularly on your left hand. But if you don't feel anything, keep trying with your hands as relaxed as possible. Try invoking a different angel, and see what happens with that one.

Practise doing your invocations wherever you are and whenever you feel like doing it, until the whole idea of talking to the angels becomes second nature to you.

This exercise is only a means of training. Once you have got the idea, gradually you will find that you only need to say the angel's name once (even mentally) to feel the energy flowing around you.

Always thank the angels.

If you are inclined to rush in 'where angels fear to tread', Zephon, the angel of awareness, comes to protect and watch over you.

Zephon has this message for you:
I am the angel whose myriad golden eyes are ever alert to care for you and whose vigilance is unceasing and eternal. My golden energy is your secret armour as my love enfolds, protects and watches over your progress. If you are one who acts first and thinks afterwards, you may call on me for support, for my golden eyes of watchfulness see all and guide you to greater awareness of situations.

If you need Zephon's watchfulness, invoke the angel by saying:
"Zephon, Zephon, Zephon, please watch over me with your golden eyes, and guide me in awareness of what I am doing*, as I wish to act only for my highest good. In love and light, love and light, love and light."

* Or you could substitute *"as I feel I need your protection"*.

Why not make a positive affirmation with Machidiel if you need more confidence or motivation? If not exactly right you can change some of the words to make them more suitable.

For confidence in determining new goals: *"Machidiel, I deserve the chance to achieve my ambitions in order to find contentment. With your help I shall clarify my new goals, ensuring they meet my real needs instead of just my perceived wants, and build the self-confidence I need to follow my dreams."*

For enthusiasm, motivation, assertiveness: *"Machidiel, I know I can have the enthusiasm and energy combined with motivation to actually achieve my life goals. With your loving support I shall assert my needs to those who count, for this will be the first step to finding real and lasting happiness."*

You can add Aries colours or crystals to further empower your affirmations (see opposite).

Aries colours boost assertiveness, enthusiasm and passion.

Hahlii, angel of colours, tells us that Aries colours are fiery and range from gold to amber and orange, scarlet, ruby and crimson. Wear red colours for assertiveness, confidence and individuality, and to bring passion and energy to power you forwards. Red is also for courage and is a colour for Camael, ruler of Mars (Mars rules the sign of Aries).

Positive gold and creative, passionate orange. Gold is for the aspect of self that helps you to make decisions and take actions in life. Orange is the colour of passion, i.e. for sexuality as well as for new ideas/innovation, creativity and transformation of self as well as life.

To dream your new goals. Place a crystal under your pillow when you go to bed, to aid Machidiel to guide your dreams about your life goals. Choose from ruby, bloodstone, garnet, goldstone or carnelian.

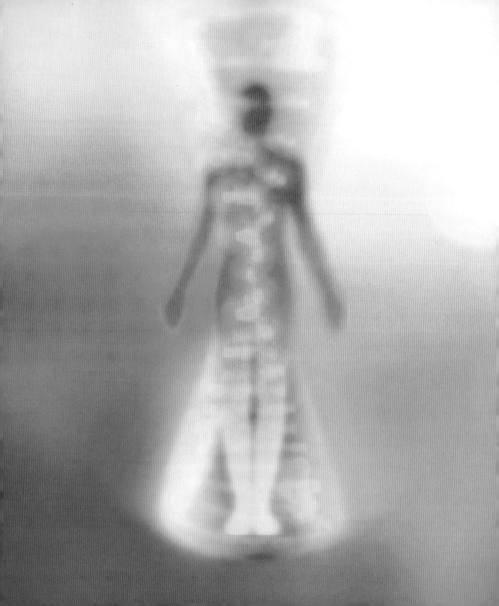

Raphael offers help with sun (also fire) energy. Sun energy aids you to make the right decisions on goals and take appropriate actions).

* Close your eyes and begin taking deep breaths of pure, white energy, breathing out any negative emotions, until you start to feel relaxed.
* Then invoke Raphael like this: *"Raphael, Raphael, Raphael, I ask for the power of sun to flow down into me from above, healing and balancing my energy and empowering my decisions. In love and light, love and light, love and light."*
* Now imagine that a golden spiral of light energy comes down from the sun and through the crown of your head.
* As this warm energy flows through your energy centres, it heals and strengthens each of them.
* Breathe this deep down into your body and visualise it energising the solar plexus area, which is where your will power is located.
* As you hold this breath say: *"Raphael, please help me to use this golden energy to determine my best way forward in life. I wish to make the decisions about goals that will be for my highest good."*
* As you breathe out, the golden spiral continues to flow down through you and out of the base of your spine, where it grounds in Mother Earth.
* This gives you a firmer foundation upon which to work.
* Always thank the angels for their help.

Aries is a fire sign; elemental angels offer tools to aid focus.

A message from Anahita, angel of medicinal plants:
Long ago man knew and understood my medicinal plants and processed their leaves or flowers to make many healing infusions and oils. In your scientific age do not forget this ancient knowledge, which still has its place. Bring my wisdom into your life with one of my remedies, to soothe and heal mind, body or spirit.

For some calmness if you have too much energy: Anahita suggests you could try drinking a peppermint tea infusion, as mints are Aries herbs, or you could use a mint, camomile or lavender oil in an oil burner.

Plants, trees and flowers, reminders for Machidiel and Aries. Red and yellow blooms generally are very appropriate. Hawthorn, fir, mint and thistle are special plants for this sign – make a small arrangement to remind you to call on this month's angels and/or address relevant issues.

Candle, symbol and fire power. As this is a fire sign, a candle can aid you this month, especially with a symbol on it. If you have a candle in red, orange or yellow (or white can always be used) draw on it the Zodiac sign for Aries (see pages 86–7), saying Machidiel's name three times as you light it. Use this during any exercises and rituals you feel you want to do from this chapter.

If you need courage to be original. Need a quick lift of inner strength? Buy a red flower or an accessory (a scarf or piece of jewellery) and place it somewhere (or wear it) where it will be constantly in your vision. It will be a reminder to ask in your heart for Camael, angel of Mars, to send you courage and empower you. See also other exercises in this chapter for confidence and re-kindling passion.

Machidiel and Mumiah, angel of wellbeing, aid you with positive energy/dynamism for a particular event or situation.

Energising your day. On a day when you know you particularly need to sparkle and speak out, invoke Mumiah as follows: *"Mumiah, Mumiah, Mumiah, please be with me throughout today to bring me the energy and enthusiasm I need. In love and light, love and light, love and light."*

Feeling depleted of energy? Sit quietly and prepare to say the name of Mumiah (angel for wellbeing) three times. Each time you say it, breathe in as deeply as you can, imagining that with Mumiah's name and assistance you are actually breathing sparkling energy and wellbeing right into your body. The power of three and Mumiah's name truly help.

To feel more dynamic about the future. Say: *"Machidiel, Machidiel, Machidiel, please bring me the power and dynamism I need to identify and achieve my real aims. In love and light, love and light, love and light."* Keep saying it daily until your plans begin to bear fruit.

Angelic assistance for heated situations, i.e. when you are too assertive or outspoken.

If you are inclined to 'fly off the handle'. Phaleg, angel of anger management, has this message for you: *You are a person who has powerful emotions, mostly positive but sometimes negative. Your passion for life itself is strong and empowers yourself and others, for when it burns from within your very soul it inspires and achieves so much. However, when that same passion leads you to be too headstrong to listen to advice, seek my aid for your highest good.*

Help from Phaleg. If you need Phaleg to help focus your emotions correctly, call on him by saying: *"Phaleg, Phaleg, Phaleg, please be with me to re-channel the angry emotions I feel now into a positive cause and outcome. In love and light, love and light, love and light."*

Violet flame bowl. You can also transmute anger or other negative emotions with the wonderful violet flame bowl, see page 77 for details.

To cleanse a room after harsh words. After an argument cleanse the room by invoking Melchisadec as follows: *"Melchisadec, Melchisadec, Melchisadec, please cleanse this room with violet fire. In love and light, love and light, love and light."* You may actually be able to feel the atmosphere in the room become lighter. Always thank the angels.

If you are going into a negative situation. Adapt the above invocation by holding a small amethyst crystal in your left hand and saying: *"Melchisadec, Melchisadec, Melchisadec, please help me use this crystal to transmute the negative atmosphere I am entering, for my highest good, highest good, highest good."*

Then carry the crystal until your meeting/task is finished and later cleanse it three times in cold running water.

Strength for individuality. If you need the physical strength to be yourself, invoke Zeruch (the arm of God) by saying: *"Zeruch, Zeruch, Zeruch, I need to be able to stand firm and find the freedom to be myself. Please help me with this strength. In love and light, love and light, love and light."*

Orange is the fire of passion, both for love and to transform life itself. Fire angels offer orange power for your new life goals.

Nathaniel, a fire angel, offers you this message:
I am the fire of passion that, once ignited, burns within you with a pure gold flame. This is fire of alchemy that brings about inner transformation. Like the phoenix reborn from the sacred flame, I help you emerge triumphant from the power of inner fire, unafraid to seek new challenges or horizons in your life.

To re-kindle sexual passion you have lost: *"Nathaniel, Nathaniel, Nathaniel, please bring back the fire of sexual passion to my life, and help me to use it wisely and with deep love, for the highest good, highest good, highest good."* Say this at the point at which you need passion.

For the passion to seek new challenges: *"Nathaniel, Nathaniel, Nathaniel, let the strength of your fire fill me with new passion to seek fresh challenges in my life, to achieve my true life purpose. In love and light, love and light, love and light."*

Camael, ruler of Mars, invites you to try this exercise. Part of this month's message is to think 'red', the rich colour of rubies. This is the colour that brings you the courage, energy and confidence to empower yourself to achieve your new goals.

- Close your eyes and start taking deep breaths of pure, white energy, breathing out frustrations until you start to feel relaxed.
- Imagine that within you, at the base of your spine you have a deep-red flower bud, and if this flower is activated it opens out to radiate light. Invoke Camael by saying: *"Camael, Camael, Camael, please bring me the power of red to build energy and confidence within me, empowering me to achieve my goals. In love and light, love and light, love and light."*
- Imagine that above you Camael is pouring deep, ruby-red light into the crown of your head.

- As you breathe in, the light flows
down and into the flower at the base
of your spine, making it open out and
glow with rich ruby light.
- From this flower the light radiates
throughout your body expanding your
feeling of strength and vitality and contributing
to your sense of security.
- As you breathe out the ruby light it creates an aura
in the shape of wings, which surrounds you with new
resolve. Ask Camael to help you lock in this
resolve, remembering to thank him for his
loving assistance.

NB: You can ask for red at this time to allow you to
feel forgiveness if you need it to assist you in your goals.

Wearing red with Camael for confidence

My son, who is an Aries, recently took his driving test for the second time and was understandably nervous. He also needed confidence as his father passed the first time and both his sister and I passed second time – he didn't want to be the only one to have to take his test more than twice. In short, this was a big thing in his life.

The test was mid-morning on a Tuesday, the day of Camael and the colour red, for courage and empowerment. I rang him the night before and told him to wear something red to take the test. I promised to do a meditation for him on the Tuesday morning invoking Camael (ruler of Tuesday) and Machidiel (for confidence, energy, enthusiasm), plus Rikbiel for power of love to triumph. Of course, I asked for all the angels to be with him during the test as long as it was for his highest good (this is very important, as it may not have been in his highest good to pass the test at that time).

Afterwards he rang us in jubilation. He wore something red, felt confident and courageous and, guess what? He passed.

I used this invocation:
"Camael, Camael, Camael, please be with my son on this your special day to give him courage, and to empower him to pass his test so long as it is for his highest good, highest good, highest good."

The amazing powers of Rochel

When my daughter Fleur graduated from university, she was broke and needed to find permanent employment as quickly as possible. She was offered two days work in London, but could not afford the train fare, so her dad purchased a ticket for her and gave it to her. That night she went out to see friends. Early the next morning she could not find her rail ticket anywhere and was in floods of tears. I told her that she would have to buy a second ticket, and that I would ask Rochel's help. This I did, and though I also searched Fleur's room and the house, there was no sign of the rail ticket.

That afternoon I decided, on the spur of the moment, to walk down to the shops for some fresh bread. As I got towards the town I reached the area where there are usually shoppers' cars parked by the pavement. Strangely, there were no parked cars, and as I neared the end of the road there was a rail ticket, face up, in the gutter. It was Fleur's ticket. Had the parked cars been there they would have obscured the gutter and I would not have found the ticket. If it had rained the ticket would have been obliterated, but as it was, I retrieved the ticket and took it to the station where it was refunded (only possible on that day). That evening I was able to give Fleur the money back for the second ticket! Thank you so much, Rochel!

See pages 233–6 for other ways Rochel can help.

April/May

Simplify your life by learning when to hold on and when to let go.

Tual, angel ruler of Taurus

My wings of love and light are filled with the strength and patience of my sign. I herald your reawakening, for my positive energy guides you to start reviewing and simplifying your life. First I bring you greater stability to strengthen your roots and foundations in Mother Earth so that you can build confidently and securely on them. Next consider your possessions – which of them do you really need and which should you relinquish? Do not over-burden yourself, for this hinders your expansion of mind, body and spirit. Therefore think of the freedom to be gained by letting go of things or learning to sometimes say no. This will give you the time to allow my green and pink, the colours of the power of the heart, to flow in; these help you to focus calmly on what is really important for your future.

Taurus, an earth sign, is ruled by Venus, planet of love and beauty. Haniel is the ruler of Venus.

Tual and the other angels feel that though you are strong, capable and caring, you may be trying to shoulder too much in life or control too many things. One way or another this is weighing you down. Whether this applies to people, burdens, possessions or a mindset, it comes down to being able to say no or let go for your own highest good. Angels of this chapter urge and aid you to think things through calmly, take stock of your life and start making some major decisions. Haniel says that love can heal and solve all issues and that inner peace is the answer.

On the opposite page, there are three headings featuring words to help you focus your needs from the angels. If any of these words resonate, then read on, as the angels of the chapter offer you appropriate assistance.

*Personal qualities linked with Taurus
and Tual:*
Patience, calmness, capability
Stability, security, responsibility

Elemental angels offer these earth strengths:
Nurturing your roots for strong foundations
Learning peace through nature's magic

*The ruling planetary angel (Haniel)
influences:*
Love and joy in relationships
Ability to have enough love to let go or say no

An invocation can get you started with Tual on one of your issues.

You will have looked at the list of qualities on page 111, to determine if any of them are linked to issues you are dealing with in your life at the moment. If so, decide your priority, in other words the personal quality with which you need angelic support. Now you can turn this into an invocation: *"Tual, Tual, Tual, please help me with my (insert the word you selected, e.g. patience or calmness). In love and light, love and light, love and light."*

When you first make your invocation close your eyes (to focus on what you can feel rather than see) and hold out your hands in front of you (palms up is good) to try to feel the angel's response.

Opposite are ways in which angels usually manifest their presence, but you may develop your own response to their comforting energy.

Your response is likely to vary according to which angel you are invoking (as each one will feel slightly different). If you start with this invocation to Tual, you will be able to monitor Tual's energy.

It's usually a feeling of warmth, gentle pressure, or tingling, and often more on the left hand than the right to begin with. This is because the left hand is considered the hand that 'takes' in terms of universal energy, while the right hand 'gives back' to the universe.

Memorise your invocation and keep saying it. Practise talking to other angels in the chapter and feeling their response or signature, i.e. how they differ from each other. Start bringing angels into your life every day and always remember to thank them for coming when you call.

In this earth sign month, Aratron, angel of nature's magic, comes to offer assistance with feeling patient and a sense of inner calm.

Aratron sends you this message:
See my mystery in the stars of the night sky, and their effect on the life of man. I reveal my powers in the beauty of silver raindrops on a spider's web, on the bark of a tree and in the haunting sound of the rhythm of drums. Is it time to let some of my magic into your life?

Invoking Aratron. If this resonates with you, call on Aratron to reveal more by saying: "Aratron, Aratron, Aratron, *please guide me in finding the magic of nature that will help enrich my own life with more patience, calmness and inner peace. In love and light, love and light, love and light.*"

For further ways in which help can be sought from Aratron, see pages 70–71 and 116.

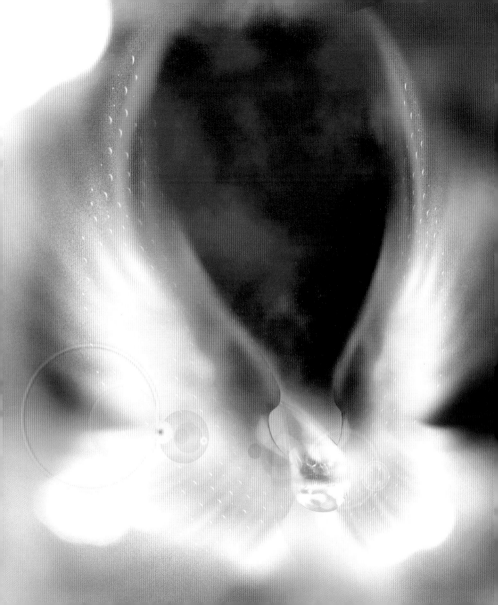

Working with nature's magic.

To find out more from Aratron. Sit quietly in a beautiful place of nature and close your eyes. Say the invocation on page 114 in your head and see what happens. You may seem to see a flash of light in your mind, or hear a message, or feel a warmth, tingling or whoosh of air. This is Aratron telling you that nature's magic could profoundly affect your life in some way.

If you have felt a response when calling on Aratron, trust this angel for further guidance. Synchronicity will start to offer you opportunities to find out about whichever aspect of magic of nature can help you. It is your choice then whether you follow these opportunities.

Plants, trees and flowers for Tual and Taurus. Violets, foxgloves, roses, daisies or apple, pear or cypress trees (cypress eases all types of transition in life) are all connected with this sign. Nature magic could involve flowers, oils, trees, crystals, metals, sound, herbal medicines, etc.

Some suggested affirmations with Tual for a Taurus issue.

To become more patient and calm, or less judgemental: *"Tual, from now on I will be more patient and calm with myself and others, as letting go of judgement will increase my tolerance and bring me greater peace of mind."*

Not taking on too much: *"Tual, I will no longer become over-burdened with other people's issues. From now on I will send them unconditional love to support them in dealing with their own problems, as I know the experience they gain will ultimately be for their highest good."*

To become less acquisitive: *"Tual, I know that I have loved acquisitions and possessions too much and with your support I now let go of this need – whether it is for people or things – in order to start simplifying my life."*

Greens, pinks and browns aid love, joy, security and stability.

Taurus colours to wear this month. The main colours to aid with Tual's particular issues are emerald, pink and chocolate brown. Taurus is ruled by Venus whose colours are the pinks and greens.

Emerald green is for calmness. It heals your emotions and heart, allowing it to open more to love so that it can be filled with the pink colours. The deeper the colours, the deeper the emotion will be.

Shades of pink build more love, contentment and compassion in the heart as well as enabling you to realise your true self-worth. With enough love you can let go of what you no longer need, to build self-esteem.

Rich brown shades are grounding, strengthening your roots for more stability and security and helping your sense of responsibility.

Crystal reminders to resist temptations. Taurus crystals can be carried or worn as a reminder to ask for help on Taurus issues – particularly if you are tempted towards retail therapy with money you can't afford. Tual's all-purpose stones are clear quartz crystal or diamond. Or you could use emerald, malachite or tourmaline. Rose quartz aids the heart. Tiger's eye quartz is good for grounding. Optionally, use crystals mentioned in the chapter meditations.

Metals and their earth energy. Taurus is ruled by Venus, and the metal for Venus is copper. For relationships, love issues and contentment, the energy of copper, perhaps a bracelet or small piece of this metal, may help to empower any exercises or meditations you do in this chapter.

Ariel, angel ruler of earth, helps with the security you need to underpin your sense of responsibility. Ariel assists you to draw in the strength of earth itself that stabilises and nourishes your roots.

- Take a piece of paper. Write down what you are resolved to do next in your life. You will hold this in your left (taking from angels) hand.
- Find a place in nature where you can stand on the earth or grass, or if this is impossible, imagine that you are doing this.
- Stretch your arms up parallel above your head, as high as you can.
- Invoke Ariel, saying: *"Ariel, Ariel, Ariel, I link myself to air and earth. Be in me, be with me, be part of me and I of you. Help me to set down new roots from my feet to ground and empower my resolve. Let these roots and the nurturing power of earth give me the stability and security I need to underpin my responsibilities. In love and light, love and light, love and light."*

\~ Imagine roots from your feet down into Mother Earth, and feel earth sending nourishment into your feet to strengthen these roots.

\~ Let this nourishment flow up to fill your heart with confidence.

\~ Let go of your self-doubts, sending them up and out through your fingers, particularly of your right (giving) hand.

\~ Complete this exercise by burying the paper containing your resolution in Ariel's earth, to complete your resolve.

\~ You can also do the emerald breathing exercise with Tual on page 125, as this builds on your foundations to bring in emerald green for calmness and to open your heart.

An angel to help you balance your income and lifestyle.

Vasariah is the angel for financial issues, and sends this message for you to take on board:

Mine is the shining ray that brings financial astuteness, an enabling energy to repair and reinforce your chalice of life. If you do not face and tackle your money issues, the beautiful gold of joy and contentment will be dissipated. Invoke me to help you with this so that the chalice can overflow once more with golden abundance. Apply as much energy as possible if you need to do this for your own highest good.

Call on Vasariah like this: *"Vasariah, Vasariah, Vasariah, please help me to address my financial issues so that with your loving support I can put my life in order. In love and light, love and light, love and light."*

Tual brings emerald green to calm, open and expand your heart, building on foundations in Mother Earth.

- Sit comfortably. Hold a Taurus crystal (see page 119) if you can.
- Close your eyes and take deep breaths of pure, white energy, breathing out any negative emotions, until you start to relax.
- Invoke Tual: *"Tual, Tual, Tual, please bring me the power of emerald green to calm, open and expand my heart, infusing mind, body and spirit. In love and light, love and light, love and light."*
- Imagine that Tual is pouring emerald light into the crown of your head.
- As you breathe in, the light flows from crown to base of spine.
- Send this light into Mother Earth, where it flows to her heart.
- Now as you breathe in, Mother Earth sends back rich brown earth energy to your feet and body, giving you a sense of belonging to all life.
- Now say one or both of these affirmations, as appropriate:
- *"With power of love and brown I form firm foundations in earth."*
- *"With power of love and green I build on these and all things become possible in life."*
- On the next out-breath breathe out the green light so that you create a coloured aura the shape of green wings, sealing in the resolve you made with these affirmations.
- Thank Tual and ask him to seal this energy into your crystal (if used); keep the crystal by you to remind you of what you are trying to achieve.

Using the colour pink for love, with Haniel, angel ruler of Venus.

Wear pink for love and joy. Haniel reminds you that pink is the colour of love, joy and compassion (including for yourself), so if you wear pink you will be able to focus on these wonderful feelings. All kinds of pink can be used, from pastel to deep rose or magenta. The deeper the colour, the deeper the feeling that can be engendered, from gentle love with pale pink to deepest compassion and unconditional love with magenta.

If you don't like wearing pink, you could purchase a small rose quartz crystal, or choose tourmaline, kunzite or a pink that attracts you. Carry or wear it when you want to be reminded of love or to promote healing of the heart. If you are wearing your crystal, choose a chain that will place it between heart and thymus for maximum effect.

Copper is the metal of Venus and love.

For thoughtfulness in love. Haniel is also a good luck angel, so double benefit here. If you are embarking on a new relationship and want to say and do the right things, wear something to remind you of Haniel.

Haniel says:
My metal is copper containing power of love; wear or carry a piece of copper to guide your loving thoughts and words and to bring my energy into your every-day life.

Place your pink crystal or piece of copper on a mirror. This magnifies the energy of your crystal and metal manifold. If you are looking for a partner, ask Haniel from your heart, saying: *"Haniel, Haniel, Haniel, please help me to find my true love and life partner, for my highest good, highest good, highest good."*

You might even catch a glimpse in the mirror of the person with whom you will fall in love!

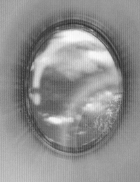

Taurus is ruled by Venus, the planet of love and beauty. If you find it hard to let go, or to say 'No', try this meditation with Haniel, angel ruler of Venus, using Haniel's pink mirror of love.

⤙ Sit down and close your eyes, ensuring that you are comfortable.

⤙ Imagine you are seated before Haniel's pink mirror of love.*

⤙ First call on Haniel by saying: "*Haniel, Haniel, Haniel, please be with me as I breathe in the power of pink and love. Help me to let go of whatever I need to in life for my highest good, highest good, highest good.*"

⤙ Now start breathing as deeply as possible, imagining that with each breath you are drawing in rose pink energy right down from your head to the base of your spine.

⤙ On the out-breaths try to release your feeling of worry for the angels to disperse.

⤙ When you feel brimming with pink energy, imagine you can send your consciousness from your head into your heart.

⤙ You are asking for help out of the love in your heart, for you wish to harm no-one by your action.

- Ask Haniel to reflect back to you from her mirror of love who or what you should be letting go of (or saying 'No' to), for your highest good in future. This may be a person or people, a possession, a burden or a mindset. Whatever you glimpse in your mind intuitively *in the next few seconds* (or you sense in your heart), will be what you need to try and address.

- Accept this and don't try to rationalise what you seemed to be shown or told in the mirror, as you are then involving the head instead of the heart.

- Thank Haniel for her assistance.

* A pink mirror that reflects anything and everything back to you, but filled with the power of love (see my previous book *A Harmony of Angels*).

Angels and unconditional love

"I had got to the stage where I felt my life had become unbearable, almost to the stage of thinking, 'What's the point?' I got dragged along to hear Angela McGerr speak, and it struck a chord with me, so I found myself buying A Harmony of Angels, Angela's first book.

"Then I was home again, alone, in the dark – just me and those thoughts – and I couldn't sleep, so I thought I might as well have a look at the book. The page fell open on Camael. And there he was – 'angel of justice and empowerment' – and I thought, 'I definitely need some of that.' So I carried on, and the next page it fell open at was Haniel, for 'healing of love', and I knew I needed that big time.

"I read how to ask for help by invoking angels, and this is what I said: 'Help me. Put me back on my feet and I will move forward, but please don't leave me feeling this miserable any more. I give up, I surrender, I really can't do all of this on my own.'

"All of a sudden the angels were there: I felt warm, and cosy, and cherished, and happy, and joyous, to the point where I knew that this must be what heaven feels like. Like a huge bear hug, and while you are in that hug you know you are safe and protected, and most important of all you are loved and never alone.

"Then, it felt as if an icicle was being drawn out of my heart, and the gap where it had been being gently closed. My heart felt as if it would burst it was so full of positive things, and I knew that I had only to trust and all would be well. A year on, I have found the Way of Love and Light. I am happy, and I invite angels to be with me every day as an integral part of my life. They have a purpose for me; I wasn't supposed to give up. And yes, everything else is working out for the best too. I am content."

(from Alison Greensmith, Hampshire, England)

Integrating heart and head for more effective relationships.

Ambriel, ruler of Gemini

I offer my powerful lavender-blue air energy to bolster your intuitive skills in solving problems, aiding you to resolve your own outstanding issues in the best way. Listen to your heart, for the answer to all you need to know will lie there. You have the intelligence, flexibility and enthusiasm to do almost anything you choose in life but sometimes you do not stop to consider how much you are taking on until it is too late. Also, you are caring and loyal, displaying great skill in communicating with others but sometimes being drained by your efforts to be a good listener. There is much I can suggest that will be of assistance. Ask for my aid with pink for heart and love and blue for head and truth to balance your decisions and wrap yourself in Michael's cobalt blue to protect and conserve your precious energy.

Gemini, an air sign, is ruled by Mercury, planet of personal truth. Mercury's ruler is Michael, angel of strength and protection.

Ambriel advises that your loyalty, sympathy and problem-solving skills are appreciated by all, but urges you not to let these be detrimental to your own wellbeing. With angelic help you can blow away stale situations and replenish your energy reserves. Also, you have many interests, but can spread yourself too thinly on occasions, or take on more than you should, often because you are not integrating your thinking between head and heart. Michael offers his protection in future and the angels in this chapter aid you with balancing these aspects of self.

Opposite you will find the key attributes for this sign. If any of these are qualities you could do with just now, or if you have too much of one of them, then this chapter will certainly be of help to you.

Personal qualities linked with Gemini and Ambriel:

Adaptability, flexibility, loyalty, balance
Intelligence/sympathy in problem-solving

Elemental angels offer these air strengths:

Air energy to replenish your vitality
Healing power of the winds, and of oils/essences

The ruling planetary angel (Michael) influences:

Strength, protection, communication and truth

On this page you will find how to start working with Ambriel to strengthen one of these personal qualities.

First, view the list on the previous page and try to decide on your priority. Is there a word or phrase there that meets your needs? Now, turn this into an invocation: *"Ambriel, Ambriel, Ambriel, please help me with my (insert the word or phrase you selected, e.g. adaptability and flexibility). In love and light, love and light, love and light."*

If you hold out your hands in front of you and then close your eyes before you say the words, you will focus on what you are feeling rather than seeing (vision is the strongest of the senses). Relax your hands and wait a few seconds to try to feel the angel energy you are invoking.

This is the type of invocation the angels taught me to teach readers, and you will find variations of this throughout the chapters.

Generally, the response you will feel is tickling or tingling on the fingers, though many people feel warmth in the palms, or soft, gentle pressure. When teaching, I have found that individuals often feel something slightly different on their hands or arms. Some people feel a rush of energy through their body, or in their heart.

If you learn how to invoke various angels, you will find that each one will give you a slightly different response, or signature. After a while, you will only have to say the name of the angel in order to feel your personal response or angel signature.

Keep talking to the angels and remember always to thank them for their presence.

As Gemini is an air sign, Ruhiel, angel of the winds, blows away the old, refreshes you and positively invigorates your spirits.

Ruhiel says:

I am the power of the winds of change. You may choose the cool east wind to cleanse and invigorate you, blowing away that which you wish to release from your life, while my westerly wind refreshes and lifts your spirits. Or you may choose the power of my warm south wind to surround you with energy and vitality, enabling you to develop your positive qualities.

If this is something you need, invoke Ruhiel by saying: *"Ruhiel, Ruhiel, Ruhiel, please bring me the power of east wind to give me release from something past (or a current stale situation, whichever is appropriate to you). Help me to lift my spirits with your gentle westerly wind, so that I can take a fresh look at life, and empower my positive qualities with your south wind. In love and light, love and light, love and light."*

To use the north wind (for removal of old behavourial patterns), see page 243.

Some affirmations to try with Ambriel (you can vary these to suit your own purpose). Make your chosen affirmation daily until you feel things changing.

To communicate more effectively: *"Ambriel, I deserve the power of clear and effective communication at home and at work. With your loving support, I know I can build this strength in myself to safeguard my future."*

For loyalty in problem-solving, without detriment to yourself: *"Ambriel, I am always willing to help others with my listening and counselling skills; from now onwards, with your loving energy and protection surrounding me, I shall not be drained by my efforts, while remaining loyal to those I wish to help."*

For protection from negativity/energy draining: If you do tend to feel drained after listening to other people's troubles, see also the meditation with Michael on pages 152–3 of this chapter.

Hahlii, angel of colours, advises on Gemini colours. Gemini colours are shades of blues, from sky to cobalt or royal, plus pinks and mauves, with crystals in the same shades (sapphire, amethyst, rose quartz).

Gemini is ruled by the planet Mercury and the angel Michael. Mercury colours are sky blue for communication skills and cobalt blue for protection with blue or yellow topaz (a fire crystal). Combine pink for love and blue for truth to make mauve, the colour of air energy in this air sign month. You can of course use other colours as well.

Plants, trees and flowers for Ambriel and Gemini. Hazel and other nut trees are Gemini trees. Use them or their fruits to remind you to call the angels or make affirmations. Gemini plants are ferns, lily of the valley, lavender, marjoram and myrtle. See also pages 142–3 for Gemini oils and essences.

In this air sign month use oils, essences and feathers to aid you.

Achaiah, angel of nature's secrets, says:
Use the power of love to invoke me and to find ways of harnessing my secrets of nature. Colour, shape or perfume, the beauty and symmetry of my flowers bring joy and energise your quest for life enhancement. Flower fragrances lift heart and mind.

Scent the air with oils and essences. In this air sign month, scent a room while doing the suggested meditations; this helps to call Achaiah to aid you as well as the other angels. You can use oils or essences made from the Gemini flowers listed on page 141.

To help creativity if you have writer's block: Rosewood in an oil burner (or two or three drops floating in water) can help the ideas to flow, aided by communing with Achaiah. Say: *"Achaiah, Achaiah, Achaiah, help me to unblock my mind with your secrets of nature. In love and light, love and light, love and light."*

If you committed your heart and loyalty to the wrong person.
Place three drops of rose oil on water and allow it to scent your
room. Invoke Mupiel, angel who mends hearts, saying: *"Mupiel,
Mupiel, Mupiel, be with me now to help heal my heart, and to
understand that someone worth my love will come my way again. In love
and light, love and light, love and light."*

Feathers are communications from angels. Feathers are linked to
air and are an angelic symbol of the spiritual path. Truth and
spirituality are closely linked, so feathers guide you to consider
whether you are speaking and living your personal truth. This is
especially relevant in this month, ruled by the planet Mercury,
whose ruler is Michael, angel of truth. Look out for tiny white angel
feathers, or buy blue feathers (for Michael) to remind yourself of
your truth.

Are you so loyal, flexible and/or adaptable that you have forgotten who you really are? Ithuriel, angel of true self, shows you the way back.

Ithuriel says:
If invoked from the heart, I show you the integrated person that you really want to be. Have you tried so hard to please others that you have imprisoned your real self? I show you the way to tear down the bars you have erected and embrace freedom again. The path of your life can be viewed as a glittering crystal mountain, at its summit the golden crown of inner peace through integration of all aspects of self. The crystal faces reflect all your many talents. Catch a glimpse of the reflections and marvel at your true potential, for when you find yourself with the power of love, absolutely anything is possible.

Invoke Ithuriel by saying: *"Ithuriel, Ithuriel, Ithuriel, please bring your love and help me to find my true self once again. In love and light, love and light, love and light."* Do this until you feel things starting to change for you.

Helpful hints on health from the angels in this air sign month.

The importance of fresh air. If you feel a bit burned out, Ariel tells you to try to get into the fresh air somewhere for a while each day. Even in winter, in fact perhaps more so when the days are shorter, real light is many times better for us than artificial lighting. Also, train yourself to breathe more deeply, to draw air right down through your body, as it is breathing that powers your energy.

Are you surrounded by a negative atmosphere? In addition to the exercise with the bowl of lavender blue flame on page 148, there are other ways to absorb negative energy around you at home or at work. Carry or wear either a small amethyst crystal (transmutes negativity) or a piece of smoky quartz (absorbs negativity). Both are crystals for Ariel and carry a little magic.

Feeling frazzled? Place three drops of lavender oil in water on a burner (or use a lavender candle). Invoke Anahita, angel of medicinal plants, to bring you peace and calmness, saying: *"Anahita, Anahita, Anahita, please be with me to soothe me with the healing power of lavender. In love and light, love and light, love and light."*

The sky need not be the limit. You can invoke the angel of the sky, Sahaqiel, to help you reach upward for spiritual aspirations. Say: *"Sahaqiel, Sahaqiel, Sahaqiel, please send your loving energy to help me spiritually as I reach for the sky. In love and light, love and light, love and light."* Look skywards for signs such as angel-shaped or wing-shaped clouds to know he is there. This will work even better if you hold a piece of celestite, his crystal, when talking to him. See also page 282.

Ariel, angel of air and earth, offers you this wonderful lavender blue flame exercise if solving problems has left you feeling drained of energy.

- Invoke Ariel to be with you as follows: *"Ariel, Ariel, Ariel, please bring me the power of angelic light, the flame that cleanses, heals and revitalises. In love and light, love and light, love and light."*
- Imagine you now have an invisible bowl of this lavender blue flame, containing Ariel's magical healing powers of earth and air.
- Hold the invisible bowl in your cupped hands.
- Breathe in deeply to inhale this invisible flame, which is pure, positive energy, drawing it right down into your lungs.
- As you breathe out, with the power of your will expel the negativity that you absorbed from being a good listener.
- Keep breathing in the blue energy and breathing out negativity until you feel revitalised, then thank Ariel for his assistance.
- If you wish to protect yourself from this in future, see pages 152–3 for an exercise with Michael to breathe a cobalt blue cloak around yourself. See also the true life stories on pages 154 and 58–9.

Ambriel and Michael, ruler of Mercury, offer invocations to aid your communication and interactive skills.

To become more flexible/adaptable in your attitude to others:
"Michael, Michael, Michael, I know that in order not to hurt I must find the right things to say and the right moment to speak. Please help me with this. In love and light, love and light, love and light."

For living your personal truth: *"Michael, Michael, Michael, I realise that lately I have been living a lie, and this is making me unhappy. Please be with me now to help me find a way out of this falsehood, so that I can be content once more. In love and light, love and light, love and light."*

You could also try the meditation on page 224.

If you are inclined to be moody: *"Ambriel, Ambriel, Ambriel, I know that I am sometimes inclined to be moody and changeable towards my loved ones. I ask for your loving assistance to smooth my emotions at such times, so that people can be more comfortable in my company. In love and light, love and light, love and light."*

If you want to be less flexible in future: *"Ambriel, Ambriel, Ambriel, I have been inclined to be too flexible in my approach to others, and this has been detrimental to my own progress in life. Help me to balance this aspect of myself more appropriately in future, for the sake of my loved ones and for my own highest good, highest good, highest good."*

This exercise with Michael, ruler of Mercury, is about breathing his cobalt blue energy around you for strength and protection.

- If you have a Michael crystal (blue topaz or sapphire) hold this in your left hand, as you can programme it during the exercise.
- Close your eyes and start taking deep breaths of pure, white energy, breathing out any negative emotions, until you relax.
- When you feel filled with white energy, you are ready for the next step.
- Imagine now that you can breathe in cobalt blue, the rich colour of Michael's cloak. This is a colour that heals emotionally as well as bringing you immediate strength and protection.
- Invoke Michael, by saying: *"Michael, Michael, Michael, I need cobalt blue to strengthen and protect me. Help me to breathe in the power of this energy and keep it around me whenever I need it. In love and light, love and light, love and light."*

➤ Continue breathing and feel the cobalt blue radiating throughout your body, bringing Michael's strength to your energy centres.

➤ Ask Michael to help you send it to a cellular level.

➤ Now, as you breathe out cobalt blue light, it swirls around you forming Michael's cloak, surrounding you with an aura of energy for strength and protection from negativity.

➤ Michael will help you to seal in the benefits, and also seal the crystal.

➤ Thank Michael for his help and repeat whenever you need his protection.

Finding the unconditional love of Michael

"Before I found the angels, my life was a mess. I felt as if I was on the edge of a chasm, ready to topple in. Then Michael came and showed me that the chasm was actually a doorway to a new life. When I invoked Michael the first time, he enveloped me in his arms. I cried, as I felt my pain and confusion wash away. Since then, I've worked closely with Michael: I have managed to come off the medication I was on for a mental disorder, and my panic attacks are less frequent, thanks to Michael's cloak.

"I finally feel I know who I am, and what I am supposed to do. I have been inspired to write invocations and to make meditation bags to help others (see page 304 for details).

"Lily, my 4-year-old daughter, has also found Michael. She was too scared to sleep in her room, so I got her to invoke Michael with me. Now, every night before bed, she invokes Michael and sleeps like a baby."

(from Leitia Ravenscroft, Southampton, England)

Two specially written invocations to Michael

Protection for a loved one:
"Michael, Michael, Michael,
please be with (name of loved one) now.
Wrap them in your protective cloak
and shield them from all harm.
And with your sword,
help them to cut through the fears that bind them,
helping them to live in peace.
Thank you for your loving protection.
In love and light, love and light, love and light."

Invocation for speaking the truth:
"Michael, Michael, Michael,
please be with me now.
Help me to communicate total truth,
allowing me to be honest with others and myself.
Help me to see the truth in all situations
and not to be misled by lies,
enabling me to live a life of love and light.
Thank you for your loving assistance.
In love and light, love and light, love and light."

June/July

An opportunity to break free and let your inner voice be heard.

Muriel, angel ruler of Cancer

I am the voice of your heart, rising pure and clear from your innermost sanctum to express your feelings, for you do not always let them be heard. In such expression I aid you to find your empowerment for the future, bringing gold for greater will power, balanced by the gentle silver energy of moon and water. You may be self-reliant, kind and loving, always giving consideration to the viewpoints of those around you, but do you do almost anything to avoid discord, suppressing your own feelings? If so, you may bring trouble on yourself, for by living a lie it may lead to loneliness or worse. Contentment comes from inner calm; I help you to speak out by sending pink rays of love to your heart, showing you the way to resolve conflict in order to find your truth.

Muriel's Cancer, a water sign, is ruled by the moon. The moon's ruler is Gabriel, who brings us the silver power of intuition and aids balance with the feminine side of our personality.

We are now halfway through another year. Muriel and Gabriel wonder if you are as contented as you appear to others. Because you are quiet and self-possessed, are you concealing your inner feelings too much? Sometimes it is necessary to speak out for the sake of everyone concerned, and living your personal truth may be the only way to real happiness. In this chapter, gold energy is offered to balance the silver of the moon in the sign, and the angels suggest different ways of healing past or present, and resolving relationship issues at work or home, so that you are free to look forward.

On the opposite page there is a list of personal qualities or attributes addressed in this chapter. View this list and see if you need help from the angels with any of these.

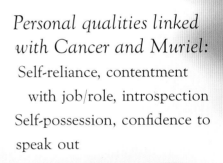

Personal qualities linked with Cancer and Muriel:
Self-reliance, contentment
   with job/role, introspection
Self-possession, confidence to
speak out

Elemental angels offer these water strengths:
The cleansing away of past issues
Lifting your spirit with oils and essences

The ruling planetary angel (Gabriel) influences:
Hopes, dreams, intuition with roles and relationships

Getting started with Muriel by making an invocation.

On the previous page you will find a list of personal qualities and attributes with which the angels of this chapter can assist you. Do any of them resonate with you? If so, help is at hand. Choose a word or phrase from the list that best meets your need, and turn this into an invocation: "*Muriel, Muriel, Muriel, please help me with my (insert the word or phrase you selected, e.g. self-reliance). In love and light, love and light, love and light.*"

When you are first making an invocation, try to allow a few minutes to reflect on what you feel when you have made it.

Sit down if possible and close your eyes (this helps you to focus on what you can feel rather than see). Hold out your hands in front of you (palms up) to try to feel the angel's response.

People's responses vary, and they differ according to which angel is being invoked. Concentrate on your hands to see whether you feel anything during the minute after you said your invocation.

Some people feel tingling on the hand, palm or fingers, but others feel energy in their heart, arms or head. It can often be rather like electricity but without heat. Sometimes there is popping in the ears. Tingling energy can also be felt in the legs and feet as it grounds you to earth.

Memorise your first invocation and keep saying it, because every time you do this you are giving it positive intent. Remember always to thank the angel.

If you want to be more confident and self-possessed, Ramiel, angel of clarity, can help.

Ramiel says:
Mine is the pure light of truth that can clarify your vision. My wings are like lenses that show a true reflection; look in them to see how you really are. I help you to recognise your own wonderful qualities, for if you can love and respect yourself you will be more confident and self-possessed. Then the next step is to let your inner voice be heard.

Invoking Ramiel. If this is how you feel about yourself, invoke Ramiel: *"Ramiel, Ramiel, Ramiel, please be with me to help me be more comfortable with myself, giving me the inner confidence not to suppress my feelings any more. In love and light, love and light, love and light."*

You can also do the short meditation with Ramiel on page 164.

Try this introspective meditation with Ramiel to see more clearly how to prioritise what you should do next in life.

- Sit down and relax a little, allowing yourself about 20 minutes when you won't be disturbed.
- Mentally ask Ramiel to be with you for your highest good.
- View the Ramiel artwork on the preceding page, for about 30 seconds, to help you connect visually to Ramiel's energy.
- Close your eyes and then breathe as deeply as possible, imagining with each breath that you are drawing in pure golden energy (Divine love) right down from your head to the base of your spine.
- On the out-breaths try to let go of your lack of self-confidence or worries.
- You are breathing out your doubts for the angels to disperse.
- When you feel calm, and filled with golden love energy, imagine that your consciousness can descend into your heart level, so that you are asking for help from a heart full of love.
- In your mind, see once again the Ramiel artwork.
- Ask Ramiel to show you in her reflecting wings, or tell you in your heart, what your priority should be for your highest good.
- Whatever you glimpse or feel in the next few seconds will be the issue you need to address first.
- Thank Ramiel for her assistance.

A choice of two affirmations you could make daily with Muriel. You can adapt these to suit your own requirements.

To be able to take a stand: *"Muriel, I know that in future I will be able to take a stand for my highest good. Help me with the intuition to know when to speak out, by bringing your loving energy to bolster my confidence, for this will be the start of my self-transformation."*

For confidence and self-reliance: *"Muriel, I know that now is the time for me to have the confidence to be my own person, and I ask for your loving support as I take these first vital and necessary steps towards self-reliance and contentment."*

Cancer is a water sign. Use water energy and nature's bounty to aid focus.

Plants, trees and flowers for Muriel and Cancer. Maples, acers and other trees rich in sap remind us about this month's issues; also, flowers in Cancerian colours, especially lilies, roses, geraniums and convolvulus, plus the herbs tarragon and verbena. As this is a water sign, oils and essences of these flowers would be excellent; either use an oil burner or float a few drops in a small bowl. This way you have both the fragrance and also the water connection while doing invocations or meditations.

Yellows, pinks and white are Cancerian. This month's colours include many different shades of yellows and pinks, from those that are almost white to the deeper colours, as well as both gold and silver. The yellows and gold help strengthen your will power, clarify the mind and bring you energy to make decisions and act on them. Pink flows into the heart, expanding it with self-worth, a love of beauty in all things and the ability to feel compassion.

Cancer is ruled by the moon and Gabriel. This means that Gabriel's cream, white and silver are also good for Cancer issues. White is for spiritual connection and silver builds your powers of intuition. Sometimes, however, a touch of gold is also required to help you make decisions and to balance the silver of your intuition. The angels offer various exercises in this chapter, according to what you need.

Crystals for the meditations from Och, angel of crystals. Milky quartz and other opalescent crystals such as moonstone and selenite are useful to increase the energy you will feel when doing moon meditations or exercises in this chapter (but do not use selenite in water). Pearls can be worn for both water and moon energy. Rose quartz helps the heart to allow self-worth, while quartz (clear or pale citrine) and rhodochrosite aid energy balance and healing.

In this water sign month Matriel, angel of rain, helps you to cleanse away something from past or present.

Matriel's message to you is:
I am the silver shower that sustains all life, for what can live without my aid? My rain also mingles with your sadness and sorrow, blending my drops with your tears so that they are absorbed and cleansed away; in every drop I hold a little of your past life. Use this powerful image to mentally wash away any issues so that with my assistance you may enjoy a fresh start in life.

Invoking Matriel. If this sounds like something that will help you, why not call on Matriel's aid? You can say: *"Matriel, Matriel, Matriel, I need your loving assistance to wash away the past and refresh the present. Please be with me to help me do this for my highest good. In love and light, love and light, love and light."*

Mentally see that you are washed clean. In your mind see yourself standing with pure water washing over you, and you are shining bright.

Using silver moon power to send loving thoughts to someone.

Ofaniel, angel of full moon, suggests doing the following on the day of full moon itself to send loving thoughts to someone.

- Use a selenite or moonstone crystal. Hold one of these crystals and close your eyes.
- Picture in your mind the person about whom you are concerned.
- Say:*"Ofaniel, Ofaniel, Ofaniel, I ask to draw down the silver ray of the full moon to my heart, to empower my intuitive thoughts with love and light. Please help me to send these loving thoughts to (say the name of the person) for the highest good, highest good, highest good."*
- Now still your mind for a few seconds, and you can send these thoughts to another at that instant in time.
- You have programmed the crystal, so keep it near you and, whenever you look at it, send the same thoughts to the one you care for.

Use the golden power of love to help resolve something.

Healing power of love. The angel Rikbiel tells you that the power of love can heal all situations.

- If faced with a situation that seems entrenched, say Rikbiel's name three times, asking him to be with you.
- Take a deep breath and imagine that you are breathing in golden sun rays of pure angelic love.
- Hold this breath asking your heart to magnify the love.
- As you breathe out, imagine that you are sending this love energy to the situation.
- Do this three times, and repeat as often as you can until the situation starts to improve.

Rikbiel says:
This breath will travel at the speed of Love to resolve and heal all problems, for whatever or wherever they may be, be assured that Love will find the way.

If you rely a bit too much on intuition (silver energy), an exercise with Diniel, a lucky golden angel, can help you be more generally decisive.

Diniel, one of the golden angels of good fortune, says:
I am with you when needed, bringing a swirl of golden energy, my bright and living light wraps and envelops you with luck, healing, balance and protection. It will also aid you to take your next decisive steps in life, those that are for your highest good.

Invoke this angel by saying: *"Diniel, Diniel, Diniel, I breathe in the power of gold. Please be with me to bring your living golden light to flow in and around me, balancing the silver within me. Empower me to be decisive and to take the right action, one that is for my highest good. Bring me luck, Diniel. In love and light, love and light, love and light."*

Do this invocation and then breathe gold around yourself, to give yourself a better balance, aid daily focus and help you to deal with something that is pending. It will form a golden cloak of light around you.

You can also send it to someone else who may need some golden assistance.

Do you act as if you are happy, but feel you are in the wrong job or role in life?

Talk to Jofiel, angel of jobs and roles. Jofiel guides you towards the role you should be pursuing with this affirmation: *"With Jofiel I affirm my need to fulfil my ordained role in life, one that brings me contentment. Please guide my steps towards this role, on a path towards inner peace."*

Dokiel, angel of balance, comes to the rescue. Do you know, deep down, that you need to make a decision about balance in life? Close your eyes and view the pros and cons, mentally asking Dokiel to add the element of love to your scales in order for your decision to be the right one in the longer term. Say: *"Dokiel, Dokiel, Dokiel, I ask for your guidance in making the correct decision about my work/life balance, for my highest good, highest good, highest good."*

When you have made the invocation you will *immediately* feel in your heart intuitively what you *should* do, but you are always free to choose what you *actually* do.

Citrus oil can lift the spirits. Why not use one of Anahita's citrus oils to lift your spirits? You could use an oil burner, float two or three drops on a dish of water or even apply a very small amount to your pulse points.

Try orange if you feel sad, or neroli (spiritually uplifting), mandarin (for happiness), or ask in your heart for guidance from Anahita, angel of medicinal plants, about which one will aid you most. Say: *"Anahita, Anahita, Anahita, please guide me in this for my highest good, highest good, highest good."*

Angelica, as the name suggests, helps to link you spiritually to angel energy by allowing you to be more in tune with your higher self.

Recite the different oils in your head, and the one you immediately, intuitively feel is right, will be right. If you know how, you could dowse with the angel Michael to find the right oil. (See *A Harmony of Angels* or *Angelic Abundance* for safe dowsing.)

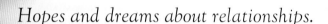

Hopes and dreams about relationships.

This is a message from Gabriel, ruler of the moon:
I come on a pure silver spiral that flows from Mother Earth to link with the power of the moon and intuition. One of my names is Awakener, for I bring you messages of fresh hope and awaken new aspirations. I also guide your dreams; you can call on me for help with relationships.

Do you need Gabriel for hope? Are you contemplating something that needs Gabriel's help? Wear something silver for the moon and Gabriel, and invoke the angel by saying: *"Gabriel, Gabriel, Gabriel, please be with me to guide my hopes and dreams about my new relationship. In love and light, love and light, love and light."*

Scrying with Gabriel to see or dream your true love.

- Take a shallow round bowl of clean water and place a small milky quartz crystal in it; the crystal needs to be fully submerged.
- Place the bowl where moonlight will shine on it (a night of full moon would be best of all) and leave it there for a full night to energise the water and crystal with Gabriel's energy.
- The next evening, in moonlight if possible, do the invocation on the opposite page, and after those words say: *"Gabriel, please show me my love, if for my highest good, highest good, highest good."*
- Gaze into the bowl for about 30 seconds and then close your eyes and see what you can see.
- If you do not see anything, place the milky quartz crystal under your pillow and mentally ask Gabriel if you can dream about your love.
- Carry the crystal around with you until you meet the person of your dreams.
- Remember to thank Gabriel for helping you.

A gold and silver sun and moon garden

"And pluck till time and times are done the silver apples of the moon, the golden apples of the sun ..." W.B. Yeats

This garden was designed by Fiona Stephenson, inspired by Angela's recent publication, *Gold & Silver Guardian Angels*. The design is based on the Vesica Piscis, a sacred geometric symbol that formed part of the cover design. The Vesica Piscis is formed when two identical circles overlap so that the circumference of one touches the centre point of the other. Each circle represents the opposite of the other. The intersection of these two circles represents harmony and balance: the common ground, shared vision or mutual understanding between two equal individuals or groups. Simply viewing this shape is said to be an experience that speaks subliminally to the soul.

The purpose of the garden is to engender a feeling of balance and harmony in a satisfying outdoor living space, an area for quiet contemplation, reflection and to promote a feeling of wellbeing. There is a deeper symbolism and allegory within the Vesica Piscis form for those who wish to contemplate more spiritual meanings within a natural garden setting.

The simplicity of form provides a balance of hard and soft landscape. The plants and flowers have been chosen not only for their easy maintenance characteristics, but also to accent the 'opposites' that the circles symbolise.

This is a garden of the sun and the moon, as well as the elements of earth, air, fire and water. In the South Circle, the sun is represented with the gold leaves and rounded form of Mexican Orange Blossom (*Choisya ternate* 'Sundance'). In the North Circle, the moon is symbolised with white flowers and the silver leaf shrub *Convolvulus cneorum*. Through the seasons, fire is represented by red flowers, such as tulips, heuchera, hemerocallis, dahlia and the purple leaves of sage and phormium. White, blue and purple flowers through the seasons represent water: hemerocallis, lavender, sage, aster and verbena. *Stipa tenuissima*, which moves in the slightest breeze, gives a feeling of movement and air. Fragrance also plays its part throughout the seasons. The red leaf *Phormium* 'Maori Sunrise', behind the red stone sphere, and the flowing grassy leaves of *Miscanthus* 'Morning Light' behind the water sphere particularly emphasise symbols of fire and water. Below is an explanation of the symbolic planting of the Vesica Piscis.

South Circle	Balance	North Circle
Individual strengths	Common ground	Individual strengths
Fire	Tranquillity	Water
Sun	Peace	Moon
Gold	Crystal	Silver
Red	Pure light	Blue
Day	Union, shared vision	Night
Masculine	Mutual Understanding	Feminine
Logic	Spiritual Harmony	Intuition

July/August

Have full confidence in your ability to lead and/or inspire others.

Verchiel, angel ruler of Leo

With the glorious strength and steadfast courage of my sign I come on my tawny wings to aid you, for my loving energy brings you the confident leadership ability to inspire truly the hearts of others with your vision. You have the potential to bring about change in the lives of many, for as well as being strong and clever, you wield the amber and gold power of the sun. This can light the fire of creativity and transform lives by introducing innovative situations in order to maximise people's potential. To have self-doubt sometimes is only to be expected, as without this you could be ruled by ego alone. My love guides you towards the knowledge you need to overcome this doubt, boosting your confidence by gradually adding wisdom of experience to your own inherent talents.

Leo, a fire sign, is ruled by the sun. The sun's ruler is Raphael, angel of healing at all levels. Raphael's golden energy also balances the masculine side of personality, bringing power of decision and action.

This month's angels urge you to bring out more of your leadership ability and inspirational qualities for the benefit of others, and they assist you with these. Verchiel says that you should not keep delaying because you feel inwardly vulnerable, which makes you reluctant to back your own hunches. There is no such thing as continual certainty. Angels aid you to be a successful and inspirational leader, who takes others forward with strength and courage, but always has a fallback plan ready to deal with the unexpected. Why not go for it? There is also a chance to find your rainbow and pot of golden energy with Raphael.

Refer to the opposite page to find the personal qualities and other issues with which the angels of this chapter can support you. Use this chapter to boost your inner confidence and to heal aspects of self that will strengthen you to achieve what you want to from life.

Personal qualities linked with Leo and Verchiel:

Courage, creativity, ability to inspire others

Leadership skills, confidence in decision-making

Elemental angels offer these fire strengths:

Cleansing, purifying, recharging of energy batteries

Rainbows of colour to enhance life/unify strengths

The ruling planetary angel (Raphael) influences:

Health/energy balance needed for positive action

How to start working with Verchiel to address one of these personal qualities or strengths.

First, identify your personal priority. Then select one of the words or phrases on page 183 that would help with this priority. Now turn this into an invocation: *"Verchiel, Verchiel, Verchiel, please help me with my (insert the word or phrase you selected, e.g. leadership skills). In love and light, love and light, love and light."*

Before you make the invocation, close your eyes so that you can focus more easily on what you can feel rather than see. Hold out your hands in front of you, either palms up or palms facing forwards, as preferred.

Say the words and then wait a moment or two, relaxing your hands as much as possible. See what you feel in response to your request to Verchiel.

This is the way the angels told me to teach people to do invocations, and 99.9% of people who call on an angel in this way will feel something in their hands or fingers, which is the angel energy coming to aid you in response to your request.

In other chapters I mention the usual ways that people feel this energy; try calling in the next angel in this chapter, Hahlii, and see how that feels. The chances are that Hahlii will feel slightly different to you than Verchiel.

Do work at it, even if you only feel the energy slightly to begin with. With practice you will gradually feel more and more. Also, the more you invite angels into your life, the more you will feel.

This is the first step of the Way of Love and Light.

Kaleidoscopes of colour enhance life and unify your strengths.

Hahlii's message:
Mine are the rainbow colours and shades of Creation, mixed on a Divine palette to enrich every day of your life. This month you have Leo's glorious fire colours of deep topaz, orange and gold to empower you to act for your highest good. Also Leo is ruled by the power of the sun, itself ruled by Raphael; this offers you the sun's unique fire that splits into the rainbow, a kaleidoscope of colour to heal you or your life issues. Each colour has its own role, but with my aid you can work towards creating the pure, white light of unity within you.

Calling on Hahlii. *"Hahlii, Hahlii, Hahlii, please bring rainbows in to heal and enhance my life and guide me on what I must do to work towards unity of mind, body and spirit. In love and light, love and light, love and light."*

Work through red and Leo shades first, as described on page 188, then move on.

Leo is a fire sign, ruled by the sun (also fire, ruler – Raphael) so Verchiel suggests fire colours this month as well as fire itself.

Hahlii offers tawny colours (see also page 186). Leo's special colours are deep topaz, amber, orange, gold and yellow. All of these colours offer courage and strength of body and mind. Verchiel colours are for lower (physical) self, and you will be guided when to move on to the heart and above. For crystals use clear quartz, amber, topaz or citrine.

Wear yellow or gold for sun and will power. Wear a piece of clothing, such as a scarf, a belt – or even underwear – that is yellow. Every time you see it or think about it you can mentally absorb the colour for more will power. Gold gives you the ability to weigh options and make excellent decisions.

Topaz, amber and orange are transformational fire colours, bringing the power of change and innovation in your own life as well as lives of others if you are a leader. All three also symbolise passion, both sexual and to achieve success in your aims.

Transformation starts with sun and rainbows.

Raphael's sun energy to lighten life:
I am the sun that lights your face and chases away the shadows. Focus on me any time to ask for the sun's rays to flow into your solar plexus. This dispels inner vulnerability and uncertainty, heals at all levels and energises your will and confidence for leadership. It also has the power to bring rainbows into your life. If there is no sun, simply will the power of the sun into yourself with Raphael's message. See also page 193 for a meditation for this.

Raphael and Hahlii advise you also to look out for rainbows. If you are calling on these angels, look out for all sorts of rainbows – signs in the sky, shining through glass or crystals in your house, or literature with the word 'rainbow' in the title regarding opportunities for work or study. All are signs that Hahlii and Raphael are with you.

Effective leadership requires health, strength and balance.

Isda, angel of food and nourishment, says:
I bring my golden energy into the food you eat to power your physical health, but if you would seek true wholeness, do not neglect your soul and your spiritual path in life, for this brings harmony of mind, body and spirit.

To ensure you have mind, body, spirit balance invoke Isda: *"Isda, Isda, Isda, please guide me to focus on what I need to do to be healthier in body, and aid my mind, body and spirit balance for my highest good. In love and light, love and light, love and light."*

You can also do the fire energy exercise on page 193.

Plants and other tools to use in Verchiel's month.

Leo herbs, trees and flowers. Bay and olive trees, and yellow or orange flowers (especially marigolds, daisies and celandines) are good this month. Plus the herbs rosemary (psychic protector, but do not use during pregnancy) and peppermint (helps to overcome inner vulnerability). You can use actual flowers, or flower essences or oils to add to the energy you will obtain doing the exercises or meditations in this chapter.

Candles for a fire sign month. A candle in a Leo colour (or white can always be used) will also add elemental energy. Inscribe the Leo symbol (see pages 182–3) on an orange or yellow candle and use as appropriate during this month. There is an orange colour breathing exercise for fire magic on page 193, and a yellow gold meditation with Raphael, ruler of the sun on pages 200–01.

A meditation for empowerment with orange fire magic and Uriel, angel ruler of fire, to cleanse, purify and recharge all the body's energy centres (chakras).

- Light an orange candle with the Leo symbol on (see pages 182–3).
- Take some deep breaths of pure, white angelic light, breathing as deeply as possible, until you feel calm and peaceful.
- Know that you have a channel, the meridian line, about two inches in diameter, running from the centre of your crown right down through your body to the base of your spine.
- Next invoke Uriel: *"Uriel, Uriel, Uriel, please be with me to bring magic of fire down the meridian line to cleanse, purify and recharge all my energy centres. I mentally release any and all blocks within me. In love and light, love and light, love and light."*
- Focus fully on the candle flame for about 30 seconds.
- Close your eyes and see the candle flame in your inner vision.
- Ask Uriel to send the essence of this candle flame in through the crown of your head at the top of the meridian line, and imagine this clear and pure flame cleansing inside your head.
- Take the flame gradually down through your body (cleansing and purifying the chakras, if you are familiar with this system).
- Imagine that the pure flame is burning away any blockages, until you reach the base of spine and the cleansing is complete.
- Ask Uriel to give you radiant wings of orange flame, to help your process of transformation.
- Ask Uriel to seal in the energy and thank him for his assistance.

Two affirmations you could make with Verchiel, if you have moments of self-doubt about your talents.

Courage to trust your own judgement. *"Verchiel, with your help I shall overcome self-doubt about my judgement and leadership skills, for I know I can be the catalyst for others to realise their own true potential."*

Vision and ambition to inspire others. *"Verchiel, with your loving support I have the vision and ambition to achieve much; aid me with the opportunity and courage to prove my creative powers and inspire others to follow."*

You could also use these as a basis to devise your own affirmation to say every day to empower your confidence.

More angelic assistance for different types of situation.

Need to clarify a situation? Sit quietly and close your eyes. From your heart invoke Ramiel, angel of clarity, to help you: "*Ramiel, Ramiel, Ramiel, please help me to see my situation more clearly. In love and light, love and light, love and light.*" There is also an exercise with Ramiel in Chapter 7, see page 164.

Regarding issues of loyalty, Icabel, angel of fidelity, says:
I give you my unconditional love without judgement or reserve and remain unswerving to you in my loyalty, whatever you do or say; this is my shining example – persevere in the spirit of love and never betray your heart.

Ponder on this message, and if you are troubled about loyalty or fidelity, close your eyes and try to see the person about whom you have doubts. Let your heart tell you what to do about it, and try to trust your intuition. See also the exercise on page 199.

For the creative ability to inspire others, invoke Radueriel, angel of artists.

Radueriel says:

I come to tell you that I, patron of artists, see that you have natural-born talent residing in your soul. It is filled with creativity that must be allowed expression, for you can take a lead to assist others to find inspiration. Be guided by your own silver powers of intuition and invoke me to support you, for now is the time for this talent to manifest.

If you want inspirational help, call on Radueriel. Say: *"Radueriel, Radueriel, Radueriel, be with me now to inspire my imagination. I know that I have this artistic ability within me. With the power of love I will find the correct medium of expression and birth it through my soul so that it inspires others. In love and light, love and light, love and light."*

See also page 199 for the silver flame bowl exercise with Radueriel to boost intuitive inspiration.

Radueriel offers you a bowl of silver flames for intuition and/or artistic inspiration.

- Use the invocation on page 196 to invoke Radueriel to be with you.
- Now imagine you have an invisible bowl of sparkling silvery flames in front of you, containing the concentrated power of silver (feminine) energy.
- Hold the invisible bowl in your cupped hands.
- Take in a deep breath of this invisible flame, which is pure silver, intuitive energy and imagine you can draw it right down into your heart.
- As it reaches your heart it kindles your powers of intuition.
- Send it also down to your lower body, to the centre for creativity and artistic inspiration.
- Keep breathing in the silver energy until you feel filled with the radiant power of its light.
- Pause and allow the angels to guide you further.
- Try to stay a while with this exercise, asking Radueriel mentally to empower you with regard to your feelings and hunches about next steps.
- Remember to thank Radueriel for his help.

Leo is ruled by the sun. Raphael, the sun's ruler, suggests this exercise with yellow-gold sun energy; this helps banish vulnerable feelings and strengthens will to clarify actions needed.

➤ Close your eyes and take deep breaths of pure, white energy, breathing out any negative emotions, until you start to relax.

➤ Then invoke Raphael: '*Raphael, Raphael, Raphael, I ask for the yellow-gold power of sun to flow into me, empowering my will and filling my mind with light. In love and light, love and light, love and light.*'

➤ Now imagine that you can take in a deep breath of this energy.

➤ Breathe this deep down into your body, and hold the breath, visualising your heart expanding this energy with love, and a bright golden star forming inside your heart.

➤ Then visualise the star within you sending golden energy throughout your lower body, particularly to boost the power of your will and mind (behind solar plexus – solar chakra).

- As you breathe out, say: *"I now expand this yellow gold star and breathe it around me."* The star will form invisibly around you, but you may be able to feel it with your fingers (it tingles!).
- Say: *"Raphael, Raphael, Raphael, please help me to use this golden energy to release my inner vulnerability so that I can take the action I need for my highest good, highest good, highest good."*
- The star is likely to last between 36 and 48 hours, after which you would need to recreate it.
- Do this whenever you need to ask for Raphael's loving assistance in decisions that will heal your life. Remember to thank him.

Raphael to the rescue

"I am a Mexican married to an American. The day I got married I had a basket full of Mexican flower seeds to remind me that I had to grow them in my new Arizona house. After some time my seeds seemed to be covered with tears – everything seemed to be lost and I felt very low. Although I didn't feel like embracing adventures in a metal bird with my two sons, the asphyxiating heat of summer convinced us to accept my sister's invitation to visit her in Mexico.

"The plane took off from Arizona, and I could feel thousands of butterflies flying around in my stomach. We were reading a book about angels but, after the airplane was shaken by an air pocket, the lady sitting across the aisle from us began to sob, then cry and scream. She was suffering a panic attack. Her companion was desperately trying to calm her down. We all turned to see what was happening, and for the first time in my life I felt trapped, in mid-air, not knowing who to turn to. I had to pretend that nothing was wrong, but the woman's terror was becoming contagious. Suddenly, I remembered what we had just read; we called out to Archangel Raphael, seeking his protection. 'Please, no more turbulence, and please help this poor woman to calm down,' we implored.

We offered our angel book to the frightened woman. With terror in her eyes, she accepted it and – extraordinarily – after a few minutes, her cries and sobbing diminished. Together we learnt how to ask the angels for help. We weren't afraid any longer: peace and harmony were within us. The woman finally fell asleep and the rest of the trip went without a problem. When we arrived, she thanked us for sharing the angel's miracle with her.

"Since then we never leave our house without Raphael. Whenever we are flying he's sitting next to us, and I can often smell the fresh scent of flowers floating in the air."

(from Nancy Alvarado, Arizona, US)

August/September

Have the ability and energy to manage life's big picture as well as the detail.

Hamaliel, angel ruler of Virgo

I am the golden summer of your life and I bring my rays of infinite love to enhance or untangle relationships. My energy smoothes your path, allowing you to move forward towards relaxation and tranquillity. First, I guide you to focus on green issues; in other words, health and nutrition, the basis for wellbeing. When you have replenished your vitality, then my loving support helps you to address any relationship matters that are troubling you. You are an excellent networker who sometimes fails to prioritise enough, or becomes side tracked. I bring you blue energy to help you to envisage and manage the whole picture of your life more clearly, instead of merely focusing on certain aspects. And I am the enabler who aids your actions and guides you to the power of truth to see all matters through to successful conclusion.

Virgo, an earth sign, is ruled by Mercury, planet of communication. Mercury's ruler is Michael, who aids also with strength and truth.

Hamaliel and the angels of this month guide you to focus first on your energy and wellbeing, to ensure that you have enough vitality for the important issues you face. From a position of strength, with Michael's backing, you can tackle relationship matters, for you have the interactive skills to enable these to run more smoothly, once you turn your attention to them. This month's summer abundance offers you also a chance for fertility – of self or new ideas. Finally, the angels offer the calm of perspective, to help to keep you on track for the big picture in life or work, instead of being bogged down in the details.

Opposite are the key words for the personal qualities this month. Have a look at these – do any of them reflect what you think you need? If so, read further, as help will be provided in this chapter.

Personal qualities linked with Virgo and Hamaliel:

    Social and relationship skills, inner tranquillity
      Conscientiousness, thoroughness, attention
        to detail

Elemental angels offer these earth strengths:

    Vitality, wellbeing and earth/crystal healing
      energy
    Fertility of mind, body or spirit

The ruling planetary angel (Michael) influences:

  Communication/networking ability, truth
and strength

Invoking Hamaliel to aid with one of these attributes.

First, consider exactly what you need from the list of qualities on the previous page. Now turn this into an invocation: *"Hamaliel, Hamaliel, Hamaliel, please help me with my (insert the word or phrase you selected, e.g. social skills). In love and light, love and light, love and light."*

Close your eyes before saying the words to focus on what you feel rather than see (vision is stronger than touch in most of us). Hold out your hands in front of you, either palms up or palms facing forwards, as preferred, and relax them as much as possible.

Say the words and then wait a moment or two. You are likely to feel something like tingles, gentle pressure, coolness or warmth – this is the angel's response to you.

Keep practising to increase your ability to feel a response.

Some longer invocations to try with Hamaliel.

To smoothe relationships: *"Hamaliel, Hamaliel, Hamaliel, I know that I need to address relationship issues at home, and with your loving protection and care I shall find the opportunity to start sorting out my problems once and for all. In love and light, love and light, love and light."*

For social and networking skills: *"Hamaliel, Hamaliel, Hamaliel, please aid me to regain my ability to talk to people I don't know, in order to be able to socialise once more. I know that I am capable of this, and used to do it well. Help me to find inner confidence once again, for my highest good, highest good, highest good."*

For conscientiousness and thoroughness: *"Hamaliel, Hamaliel, Hamaliel, help me not to rush through my tasks and to apply the necessary attention and thoroughness to what I have to do, as in the long run this will be the wisest choice. In love and light, love and light, love and light."*

Is it time for new fertility of mind, body or spirit in your life?

Yusamin, angel of fertility, has this message for you:
From the wellsprings of Love and Light I stream, on shining wings fashioned from living light itself. I carry in my heart the silver seeds of fertility and the power of love to make all things grow and flourish for the highest good. My task is to bring you fertility of mind, body or spirit; you may seek my aid according to what is for your highest good.

Invoking Yusamin: *"Yusamin, Yusamin, Yusamin, I summon you from the wellsprings of light to be with me, for now is the time for me to find new fertility of (mind, body or spirit – whichever is appropriate for you*) to enrich and expand my life. Please bring me your loving support as I pledge to undertake this new phase. In love and light, love and light, love and light."*

* mind – new ideas/plans
body – conception
spirit – spiritual development

Virgo is an earth sign. The angels of plants, crystals and nature reconnect you to Mother Earth and her many secrets.

Hahlii, angel of colours, says that special colours for Hamaliel and Virgo are greens and blues, with touches of gold and brown for the earth connection.

Virgo greens are a reminder about health. These tones are also for the expansion of body, mind or spirit and especially for healing and reopening your heart.

Mercury rules Virgo and brings the blue colours. These help your inner tranquillity and communications skills at home and at work. They aid you to choose your moments with care when working towards speaking and living truth with regard to relationships.

Zuphlas, angel of trees, tells us that trees are especially important in earth sign months as they remind you to take a longer-term view in your life. Virgo special trees are those bearing nuts, such as hazels, walnut and chestnuts.

Och, angel of crystals, offers his wisdom:
In this earth sign month I offer you energy of crystals, created from the beginning of time deep within the heart of your Mother Earth and now brought to the surface through my powers of alchemy. Use those of my crystals that call you, ensuring honesty of intent and with a loving heart, for crystal power aids change within you or your life.

Using or choosing a crystal. Crystals choose you rather than the other way around. Using crystals adds ancient earth energy and the power of the crystalline structure itself as well as the colours of the month. This month carry a green crystal for Hamaliel (choose from emerald, malachite, tourmaline) or blue such as topaz or turquoise. Use them as suggested when doing this chapter's exercises or meditations. If you need grounding/balancing, choose haematite, tiger's eye or smoky quartz.

Using Mother Earth's bounty for health, wholeness, joy and happiness.

Sofiel, angel of nature's bounty, says:

I spring on golden rays from Mother Earth, bringing you advice on how to use her nurturing fruitfulness. In this earth month I counsel you especially to consider becoming healthier, and therefore stronger, benefiting you as well as those who depend upon you. To assist you, I bring my golden philosophy containing a message of truth for you on living life wholesomely and joyfully.

Sofiel's advice:

Eat and drink wisely, never neglect this aspect of wellbeing. Reduce harmful intakes, eat wholesome rather than processed food and ensure you are consuming enough vitamins and minerals to be healthy.

Breathe properly (deeply), for breathing empowers your energy centres.

Look around you and feel joy at the beauty of nature. Let this joy radiate.

Respect Mother Earth. Love her and her bounty, respect animals and all creatures, feel your connection to All Life and reap the benefit.

Sachluph, angel of plants, brightens up your life.

To brighten your day, ask Sachluph, angel of plants, to help you choose intuitively a green leafy pot plant for your house or apartment. Every time you look at it you will absorb the energy vibration of green for growth, plus the aura of the plant itself. Or you could choose suggested plants and colours for Hamaliel and Virgo, which are daisy, forget-me-not or lavender. Colours are white, blue or yellow and again you will absorb the colour/aura while caring for the plant.

Invocation to the angel of plants: *"Sachluph, Sachluph, Sachluph, please aid the plants of home, garden and meadow to grow and flower with joy and beauty. In love and light, love and light, love and light."* Say this over a plant that needs your help.

Sachluph shows you a way to use earth power. This earth exercise with Sachluph is for self-empowerment.

- Take a little earth and place in a small bowl.
- Find a small seed, or rice grain, and plant it in the earth, just below the surface, then apply a little water.
- Now close your eyes and imagine that you are that seed.
- Really feel as if the nurturing power of earth is warming you and giving you strength and energy, aided by the water of life.
- Put positive energy into willing yourself to grow taller to reach towards light and feel your triumph as you break through the earth.
- Mentally ask Sachluph to empower the new you with the particular qualities you need this month.
- You can do this in your life – you just need enough positive intent.

A Mumiah meditation for vitality and wellbeing.

- Take in deep breaths of pure, white light, the positive energy of the angels and, as you breathe out, expel your negative thoughts, until you feel filled with white light.

- Imagine that you can be a channel for a spiral of crystalline energy to flow into you through your crown, and then down the meridian line through your body, which runs from crown to the base of your spine.

- Invoke Mumiah to help you do this, saying: "*Mumiah, Mumiah, Mumiah, help me to breathe crystalline energy through the top of my head and into the meridian line through all energy centres, bringing me vitality and wellbeing. In love and light, love and light, love and light.*"

- Imagine that this sparkling energy is flowing into your crown and, as it flows through you, try to feel it bringing energy and strengthening your immune system.

- The crystal spiral flows down through the meridian and grounds through the base of your spine into Mother Earth.

- You are now connected to Universal Source through your body, and crystalline light radiates from the meridian line into your energy centres.

- Crystal contains the potential for all colours and therefore gives you perfect energy balance and a feeling of tranquillity.

- Send love, light and thanks to all the angels.

Iadiel, angel for dispelling worry, helps you to gain perspective about things that concern you in order to be more relaxed about what to do.

Iadiel's message:
My golden wings have the power to lift you from all earthly cares, even if for just a brief moment. I suspend you in time and space like a great bird traversing a limitless sky, so that in a moment of tranquillity you can see your situation more clearly. Take this opportunity to soar mentally with me into the sky and look down from a distance on your worries and put them into better perspective.

To see your own 'big picture' call on Iadiel as follows: *"Iadiel, Iadiel, Iadiel, I ask you to help me see the entire picture and to put things into perspective, for then I shall know what to do next. In love and light, love and light, love and light."*

Try to think with heart as well as head when making your decisions.

Finding tranquillity and serenity with Cassiel after a difficult spell.

Cassiel, ruler of Saturn, reminds us that all life has contrasts and that through facing and overcoming our dark times we can gradually find harmony again and can move to tranquillity and serenity. If you have just gone through a difficult or dark period in your life it may have been caused by karmic issues you agreed to face and overcome in this lifetime. By accepting this situation, finding some redeeming aspect to the negative offered, and working through your challenge to achieve a positive outcome, you will be freed to move on.

To understand Cassiel's message better. Place a piece of obsidian and a piece of selenite side by side on your desk or table, or you could use snowflake obsidian or black-and-white agate. It is said that the darkest time of the night is just before dawn. If you are having a hard time just now, remember that as certain as day follows night it will pass.

Michael, ruler of Mercury, says:

From the wellsprings of Light on a dazzling beam of gold I travel to strengthen and protect you; my brilliance dispels all darkness and falsehood from your life.

If you have had throat problems it may mean that you have felt unable to express your true feelings. Suppressing them can result in constant sore throats or colds. Michael can help you to deal with this by offering loving support – if and when you choose to tackle the issues. You could also do the meditation with Michael on pages 224–5.

For conscientiousness and strength to speak out: *"Michael, Michael, Michael, I ask for your assistance in clearing up misunderstandings. I know that I must deal with this and it will take all my strength. Please bring me your loving support and enfold me in your strong wings, so that I am empowered to speak out for my highest good, highest good, highest good."*

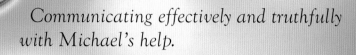

Communicating effectively and truthfully with Michael's help.

- Close your eyes and start taking deep breaths of pure, white energy, breathing out any negative emotions, until you start to feel relaxed.
- If you have a sapphire or blue topaz, hold this in your left hand, as you can programme it during the meditation.
- Then invoke Michael by saying: *"Michael, Michael, Michael, help me to breathe the power of sky-blue energy into my throat to allow better communication. In love and light, love and light, love and light."*
- Now, imagine that you are breathing in sky-blue light that fills your throat and radiates around this area, removing blocks to truth and helping you with self-expression.

➤ As this blue energy fills your throat (chakra) make this affirmation as well, if you wish, as positively as you can, to start off your quest towards truth: *"With power of blue and Michael's sword I embrace truth, wisdom and freedom."*

➤ If you had a crystal you will have programmed it during this meditation. Hold it in both hands and ask Michael to seal in your resolve.

➤ Keep the crystal by you as a reminder of what you can accomplish with this exercise; repeat it as often as you like until you find your truth.

Angelic guidance towards health and truth

"I have a story I would like to share as I was astounded by it. I regularly draw Angela's angel cards whatever I feel like each day, and they always have a message or mean something to me. A couple of months ago I drew Isda, angel of food/nourishment, and read that she helps you discover an imbalance that is seriously depleting energy and impairing your wellbeing. As I have had quite a lot of digestive problems for a few years now I know this to be true, but wondered quite how this would happen.

"I am studying homoeopathy and I opened a new Materia Medica book I had just got from college. As I did this a tiny white feather floated down and landed right next to the homoeopathic remedy heading Mandragora, at the top of the page. I was very surprised by this and a little taken aback but in homoeopathy you match the remedy picture to your health picture and this remedy seemed to fit lots of my physical symptoms. I decided to try the remedy and was amazed to find that it really helped my digestion problems. I feel so much better. I now also dowse with Michael, angel of truth, to check I have the correct remedy before prescribing it to my patients. I feel the messages I receive from the cards are truly a gift from heaven and it helps me to find the correct remedy to help people get better."

(from Rachel Durnford, Leicestershire, England)

Angel feathers

"After a four-month stay in hospital, my mum was finally well enough to be discharged but not well enough to go back to her own home. She was distressed that she would have to convalesce first. Every day I put protection around her and asked the angels to take care of her as I do all my family. My mum felt ill and rang me one day. I rushed over to find a white feather on the doorstep. My mum was starting to go hypoglycaemic.

"A few months later she wanted to go and collect some personal items from her own home, which I had also put angelic protection around due to the high number of burglaries in the area. When we got there, both neighbours either side of her had been broken into. My mum's house had not been touched despite her absence and when we got in to the house, there in the middle of the lounge were three pure white feathers. I always remember to thank the angels for their assistance."

(from Dympna Swan, UK)

September/October

Filling the scales of your life with love brings balance and harmony.

Zuriel, angel ruler of Libra

Mine is the pure golden energy that fills the scales of your life to the brim with love, to help balance and guide your decisions. When these decisions are life transforming I give you my golden eyes to perceive your higher purpose. There are always choices to be made, and I recognise that much can rest on making them correctly, but do not let life pass you by while you vacillate. If you are even now faced with a difficult decision, invoke my name and ask your heart what is best for your future. With the power of pink and rose I help you to interpret what your heart says in reply. Also, work with me to ensure that your life is in good balance, particularly in matters of career and home relationships. Lavender air energy refreshes, green soothes mind and encourages bodily health, while violet urges you to spiritual expansion.

Libra, an air sign, is ruled by Venus, planet of love. Venus's ruler is Haniel, who shows you the beauty and compassion in yourself.

Zuriel and Haniel say that this month's admirable personal qualities include straightforwardness and a general desire to conform to rules and behavioural issues, though they warn that you should not let this get in the way of any originality or individuality needed to express yourself. Don't judge yourself too harshly either. Try to maintain a healthy balanced view of your attributes, which is where this chapter comes in. If you wish, you can rid yourself of old behavioural programmes, such as a tendency to prevaricate. The angels guide you with your life-changing decisions or opportunities so that you don't miss out on anything that would be for your ultimate good.

Opposite are the key words for this month. Are any of these qualities you need, or need to have rebalanced? Help is at hand in this chapter.

Personal qualities linked with Libra and Zuriel:
Straightforwardness, conformity, decisiveness
Integration, harmony and balance in mind, body
and spirit

Elemental angels offer these air strengths:
Power of winds to remove old behavioural
programming
Oils/essences to heal and open the
heart

*The ruling planetary angel
(Haniel) influences:*
Love and compassion for self and
others

Start with aid from Zuriel to strengthen one of these personal qualities.

Decide whether you need any help from the angels of this chapter and, if so, prioritise the personal quality or strength you want to address. Now turn this into an invocation: *"Zuriel, Zuriel, Zuriel, please help me with my (insert the word or phrase you selected, e.g. mind, body, spirit balance). In love and light, love and light, love and light."*

In previous chapters I have explained how you can learn to feel the angel energy that comes in response to your invocation.

Each angel will touch you in a slightly different way, so that you get to know which is which. They may bring a fragrance or perfume, like rose or lily, which seems to come and go.

Experiment with learning how the response to angels differs by calling on Rochel, the angel of lost things, who appears on the next pages of this chapter. See how Rochel's energy feels to you. It is the effect of being able to feel angelic energy that makes many people realise that the angels are indeed there for you.

If you practise this, it will help your ability to sense the presence of the angels around you. As you become more experienced you will feel more and more, or you may even see a picture or colour in your mind's eye.

To retrieve something you had once and feel you may have lost.

Rochel's personal message:
I bring you a shining bubble of golden energy; in it you may see, if you will, something you have lost from your life. Look on this and reflect. Did you wish to be rid of it, or do you want it back? If your answer is the latter, I am here to aid you with my loving assistance.

If this resonates with you, invoke Rochel like this: *"Rochel, Rochel, Rochel, please help me to find and bring back that which I have lost. In love and light, love and light, love and light."*

The exercise on page 236 can also help in this quest. Before you try this, consider exactly what you would like to re-find with Rochel.

An exercise with Rochel to retrieve something you have lost.

- Take some deep breaths of pure, white light, the positive energy of the angels, until you feel calm inside.
- Now view the illustration of Rochel on page 235 for about 30 seconds and try to connect mentally with the angel through the power of love and light.
- Close your eyes and you will see an impression within your mind.
- From your heart, tell Rochel what it is you feel you have lost, mentally asking that you re-find it, if for your highest good.
- Rochel will try to give you a glimpse of what you should do.
- You may hear Rochel seem to tell you how to retrieve what you have lost.
- Be patient, and try several times if you find this difficult. Sometimes these processes take a little while to accomplish.
- Always remember to thank Rochel for her help.

Make a daily affirmation with Zuriel for balance in your work/life or timely decision-making.

A better balance in work and life. *"Zuriel, with your help I shall find the courage to change my work/life balance for the better. Starting from today I shall take the necessary corrective steps, as I know this will gradually lead me towards future contentment."*

Making the right decisions at the right time. *"Zuriel, I deserve not to lose out in life by failing to make the right decisions. Be with me to stop me from hesitating, as I wish to be more decisive in life from now onwards, for my highest good."*

Colours, trees, flowers and oils to aid focus on Libra heart issues.

Plants, trees and flowers for Zuriel and Libra issues. Apple, ash and maple are trees connected with Libra, as well as apples themselves. Flowers are roses, daisies and hydrangeas, particularly in the Libra colours. Use an arrangement of twigs or flowers to aid your focus on this month's issues.

As this is an air sign month, why not use rose or rosewood oil, especially for heart issues?. Rose (a Libra flower and the flower of love) has a vibration close to the angels (pure positive love energy) and helps to summon them. Rose opens the heart to love, and rosewood works on the crown chakra (top of crown), aiding you to deepen your Divine connection. As Libra is an air sign, you could use a few drops of an essence or oil to perfume a room, or apply sparingly to pulse points if doing a meditation or exercise in this chapter.

Libra colours are rose pink, green, mauve and lavender.

Libra is ruled by Venus, whose ruling angel is Haniel. Haniel brings you deep pink, the colour of compassion and unconditional or non-judgemental love, including of yourself. Pink and green are colours to aid the heart to heal and balance.

Mauve is a balance between blue and pink, connecting to the throat and the heart, leading the way up to lavender/violet – the colour of the third eye, a focus on spirituality. Lavender blue is also for the healing power of air.

Libra crystals include rose quartz and pink/green tourmaline and amethyst, although you can use crystals of similar colours if you prefer.

White feathers: indicators to look skywards towards spiritual balance and direction.

For spiritual/physical balance Alphun, angel of doves, says:
I am the angel of white doves, a symbol of your spiritual journey. If you seek my aid I will lift your consciousness skywards towards All That Is. Look out for white birds flying, tiny white feathers in your path and feather-like clouds – all are signs that I am communicating with you.

Invoking Alphun. If you need Alphun's assistance say: *"Alphun, Alphun, Alphun, I have come to the point in my life where I need your spiritual guidance. Please send me the signs and show me how to move forwards on this path of Light, for my highest good, highest good, highest good."*

If you have invoked Alphun, keep looking out for signs: a cloud shaped like a wing or an angel, doves or swans flying. You will start to find tiny white feathers. From that moment, you will know you are being guided.

A balance of gold and silver will help you to apply the right amount of intuitive thought to your decision-making.

Gold energy is brought to you by Raphael, ruler of the sun. This is masculine energy that helps with decision-making and action, but too much gold means you may rush into decisions without thinking things through. For more gold ask Raphael by saying: *"Raphael, Raphael, Raphael, please aid me with more gold so that I can make the right decision, for my highest good, highest good, highest good."*

Silver energy comes to you from Gabriel, ruler of the moon. This is the feminine energy to empower your intuition, encouraging you to give enough thought and 'gut feeling' to what you do. Too much silver would cause you to hesitate too long before making decisions. For more silver ask Gabriel by saying: *"Gabriel, Gabriel, Gabriel, please bring me silver to further empower my intuition, so that I can make the right decision, for my highest good, highest good, highest good."*

Here are ways to eradicate old patterns that get in the way of your success. Are you a person who makes the same mistakes over and over again?

Ruhiel says:
I am the breath of the four winds. Invoke my help to bring the healing element of my cold wind of the north; by will and intent this power can isolate and remove such programming from your mind.

If this message seems to be for you, invoke Ruhiel specifically to come into your life. *"Ruhiel, Ruhiel, Ruhiel, please bring me the essence of the north wind, to isolate and remove programming from my mind that causes me to make the same mistakes. Let me be released now and always. In love and light, love and light, love and light."*

For help from Ruhiel's other winds, see page 138.

To be established in strength, harmony and balance in life, you can call upon the angels of the four corners of the Universe: Gabriel (north), Uriel (south), Michael (east) and Raphael (west). This simple ritual takes about a minute only, and uses the ancient symbol of the equal-armed cross, centred in the heart.

➤ Hold out your arms, as in the illustration opposite, and do the following invocation:

"Gabriel, Gabriel, Gabriel,
Uriel, Uriel, Uriel,
Michael, Michael, Michael,
Raphael, Raphael, Raphael,
Be in me, be with me, be part of me and I of you.
Establish me in strength, harmony and balance in life,
For Eternity.
In love and light, love and light, love and light."

➤ You may be able to feel energy flow along your arms into your heart.

➤ Remember to thank all the angels for their assistance.

Libra is ruled by Venus. Haniel, ruler of Venus, offers guidance on compassionate love.

To help yourself or someone else. If your own heart is troubled (or you know someone else in that situation) you can invoke Haniel. A suitable invocation would be: *"Haniel, Haniel, Haniel, bring me your loving support to help my (or the person who needs angelic help's) heart to be healed and bring joy back into life. In love and light, love and light, love and light."*

If you want to do this invocation to assist someone else, you should always try to get their permission first; failing this, if for any reason the other person rejects your help, it will just come back to you in the form of love. Energy of tourmaline (a Libra crystal) also aids healing the heart, especially if it is pink and green, both heart colours. Give a small piece to the person you wish to help, explaining it should be carried until the heart feels soothed.

For straightforwardness of approach without judgement.

Hadakiel, an angel of justice, says:
I show you my golden scales of justice, but ask you not to confuse justice with the wrong kind of judgement. Perhaps you are too hard on yourself as well as on others? Also, you may consider yourself straightforward, but to others your views may be rigid or even intolerant. If you feel this issue needs addressing, in order to improve quality of life, call on me for aid before you speak out.

To invoke Hadakiel: *"Hadakiel, Hadakiel, Hadakiel, please be with me now to counsel me before I speak out. Stop me from saying something I may later regret, and help me to be tactful with my opinions. In love and light, love and light, love and light."*

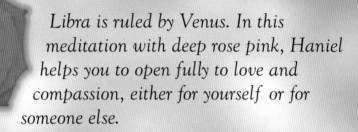

Libra is ruled by Venus. In this meditation with deep rose pink, Haniel helps you to open fully to love and compassion, either for yourself or for someone else.

🍂 Close your eyes and start taking deep breaths of pure, white energy, breathing out any negative emotions, until you start to feel relaxed.

🍂 Then invoke Haniel: *"Haniel, Haniel, Haniel, I ask you to bring me magenta-coloured light so the power of your loving compassion flows into me, comforting me, for the highest good. In love and light, love and light, love and light."*

🍂 Now imagine that you can breathe in this light and that with each breath you are breathing it deeper into yourself, towards your heart.

🍂 See your heart as a flower, such as a pink rose.

🍂 If your compassion is needed for another (or others), at this point mentally place them in the heart of the rose, amongst the petals.

- When the magenta light reaches your heart it pours into the rose and reaches the person you have placed there.
- The magenta light will then radiate from the rose of your heart into your body and spirit, infusing all with the warmth of compassion.
- As you continue to breathe this pink energy in and out it gradually forms wings of light around you.
- You may actually be able to feel this tingling energy around you.
- Thank Haniel for her help.
- Do this as often as you like to renew the magenta wings with Haniel's loving assistance.

Sadriel and Eth save the day

"I had to take an exam and because I was nervous I went early to make sure I could park my car. I did have to drive around, but eventually I found a space. I parked and crossed over a major dual carriageway that took some time to navigate across. As I approached the examination building I looked up and saw a sign that said: 'parking for one hour only'. I knew that my exam would last two hours, and I suddenly felt sick as I realised that if I went to move my car and look for another space I would be late for the exam.

"I called all seven archangels and also asked Eth and Sadriel to be with me and to look after my car while I did my exam. I did feel a bit guilty asking them to do something in a situation caused by my own incompetence. After my exam, I came out of the building to discover that all the cars on the road had penalty notices. I realised my own folly and that I would just have to bear the consequences. I crossed the dual carriageway and approached my car, but miraculously there was no ticket on it! I could not believe it – the angels were truly there for me. I hadn't thought it would really be possible to place invisible protection over my car. I thanked them profusely and suddenly a huge white light surrounded me with love and laughter. This incident always brings a smile to my face."

(from Wei Tang Phillips, Herne Bay, England)

Angels and auras

"I use Angela's CD (Angelic Meditations for Harmony and Balance) to help me meditate at least twice a week, as it relaxes me, calms me down and through it the angels help banish any negativity.

"On beginning the meditation my hands begin to tingle like very mild pins and needles. Gradually a feeling of warmth spreads down my body to the tips of my toes. By this time my body feels like it is pulsating with the light I have inhaled and is glowing in the darkened room. I sense that the angels are standing around me cleansing my aura. When I am deep into the meditation my body feels heavy as if my head has sunk into the pillow. I then begin to feel detached from my physical self; I don't seem to have the ability to move anything. My mind may tell my index finger to move but I can't physically feel myself doing it. When I am coming out of the meditation feeling comes back into my body beginning with a tingling sensation in my toes and fingers. The meditation leaves me floating on air. I feel refreshed and in a more positive mood.

"Through regularly doing Angela's meditations I have met my Guardian Angel Katherine. The more we meet through meditation the more I am able to sense Katherine in my daily life. Knowing that Katherine is around me gives me security and presence of mind."

(from Vicki Grady, Liverpool, England)

Minimising risk and maximising luck when embarking on new ventures.

Barakiel, angel ruler of Scorpio

I am the golden force that helps you to calculate chance and risk, whether in people, ventures or situations, for I bring you positive energy and luck to power your thinking and help you determine your best way forward. My guidance helps you not to waste your valuable energy in following the wrong options or trusting the wrong people, for much is either gained or lost in such circumstances. My coral and aqua colours protect you as I urge you to be calm and to ask the right questions if you wish to learn the truth, applying these questions to yourself as well as to others. To this end, mauve helps you to develop your sixth sense towards psychic perception. Remember always to think before you act, for you must maintain your integrity and rightness of actions to find lasting happiness.

Scorpio, a water sign, is ruled by Pluto, planet of mystery. Pluto's ruler is Ariel, who shows us how to pierce the veils between worlds.

This is a month for those who are considering new ventures and need to evaluate these important opportunities. Barakiel guides you in trying to minimise risks and maximise luck and possible gain. Other angels of the month suggest that it may be the right time to get off the fence, for you have considerable talents that they help to bring out. Ariel offers more psychic awareness. Angels assist you with inner healing of heart, which may be holding you back, and bring calmness of thought. This enables you to work out whether the new ventures will aid you to achieve your true potential in life.

The key personal qualities for this month are listed opposite. Take the time to peruse this list and see if any of these words resonate with you or your current needs. The angels of the chapter help you to meet those needs.

Personal qualities linked with Scorpio and Barakiel:

Astuteness, ability to evaluate situations, ambition
Realisation of your true potential

Elemental angels offer these water strengths:

Calmness of thought, healing of heart
Power of water energy to aid you in situations

The ruling planetary angel (Ariel) influences:

Psychic awareness/development
Expansion of spiritual consciousness

Working with Barakiel on your choice of one of this month's qualities.

From the list on the previous pages, decide which is your priority issue for which you would like angelic assistance. Choose the word or phrase that best meets your need. Now turn this into an invocation: *"Barakiel, Barakiel, Barakiel, please help me with my (insert the word or phrase you selected, e.g. ability to evaluate a situation). In love and light, love and light, love and light."*

In previous chapters I have explained how to invoke the angel whose help you need and how to feel the response of that angel. In this case you are seeking a response from Barakiel. Notice how this feels. Remember, each one feels very slightly different, rather like a signature.

Keep doing the invocation – better still memorise it – so you can practise often with calling in your angel of choice.

Two positive affirmations to try with Barakiel for Scorpio issues.

When you have mastered the invocation to Barakiel, you could add an affirmation to put plenty of positive energy into what you are trying to achieve. Some examples are given on this page, but feel free to amend them or make up one of your own. The important thing is to keep saying it every day, as by doing so you are encouraging positive events into your life.

For commitment to the right enterprise: *"Barakiel, with your aid I shall be more discerning in calculating risks with people and projects in future ventures, and I shall evaluate them fully and with integrity before making a commitment."*

To recognise and grasp opportunities: *"Barakiel, I shall be vigorous and decisive in considering all new self-development possibilities and not let opportunity pass me by, for my heart has the power and strength to achieve so much for the right purpose."*

*Unearth your talents and skills for ambitious new
ventures with Parasiel, angel of hidden treasure.*

Parasiel says:
*I am the bright light that shines from deep within you, the treasure of
your true talents and abilities that circumstances have caused you to bury.
The good news is that all is not lost. Within your heart is the knowledge
and love you need to find your personal treasure trove anew. Seek my aid
to focus your heart within, for it is time to unearth these talents. Have
courage, for they will enable you to take on new challenges to enhance
your life.*

Invoke Parasiel, by saying: *"Parasiel, Parasiel, Parasiel, I know in my
heart that I have buried my talents, but need confidence to retrieve them.
With your help I can relocate my hidden treasure to enrich my life. In love
and light, love and light, love and light."*

Scorpio is a water sign. Phuel and Haurvatat, the water angels, will guide you towards calmness of thought.

Haurvatat, guardian angel of rivers, tells you to go more with the flow. If you need the help of Haurvatat, you can say: *"Haurvatat, Haurvatat, Haurvatat, please help me to be more intuitive and perceptive, so that when it is beneficial I can go more with the flow in life. In love and light, love and light, love and light."*

Phuel, lord of the waters, reminds you that water is calming and soothes emotions. Say: *"Phuel, Phuel, Phuel, please bring me the power of water to calm and stabilise my emotions, for my highest good, highest good, highest good."*

Water can be used in many other ways. On page 266 you can find out more about how to use water energy to address Scorpio issues.

Haniel helps you towards healing the heart if you have trusted the wrong person.

Haniel, angel of love, is associated with coral, a Scorpio stone. If you have had a disappointment in love, buy yourself a small piece of pink coral and programme it by saying: *"Haniel, Haniel, Haniel, I ask you to help me programme this coral with the healing power of love, to soothe and mend my heart. As I carry this coral, please allow the healing process to continue until my heart is ready to open again to new love, for my highest good, highest good, highest good."*

Adding more focus. If you have a pink or pink and green scarf, and a candle of similar colours, this combines the two heart colours. Place your coral on the scarf and use a few drops of rose oil (this has a special affinity with the heart) either in a burner, or on your wrists. Light your candle, make the invocation and close your eyes. Wait for Haniel to come and assist you with your heart healing. Always thank the angels for their loving help.

How to use the reds, blues and mauves that are special to Barakiel and Scorpio.

Scorpio colours/crystals are deep red, coral, mauve and blue-green or aqua (the water connection). Appropriate crystals include ruby or carnelian, amethyst and coral. Coral is also a stone for good luck. Aquamarine is another crystal to use when doing invocations with water angels. You can also use other crystals of similar colours in exercises in this chapter.

Deep burgundy red and coral. Deeper reds aid you with the energy and vitality you need, while the orange coral offers the opportunity for change or life transformation. The latter (either the colour or stone) would be good to wear when considering new ventures or projects.

Scorpio is ruled by mysterious Pluto. Pluto's ruler is Ariel, the angel of earth and air magic. Ariel's amethyst shades help your psychic perception when evaluating people and situations, helping you to think with heart as well as with head for balanced judgement.

Scorpio trees and plants. Box, hazel and berried trees are associated with this month. An arrangement of red, coral or mauve coloured flowers, such as geraniums, asters or chrysanthemums (or others of your choice) generally reminds you to call on Barakiel and other angels in the chapter.

Essential oils for healing. You could also use any of the plants offered by Anahita on page 267 to help with healing the energy centres that are specifically connected with Scorpio colours.

To empower intuition when evaluating options, Gabriel, ruler of the moon, offers silver moon energy to boost your intuitive skills. This exercise helps with balance if you are inclined towards making snap decisions or evaluations (gold) and need to use more intuition (silver).

- Close your eyes and start taking deep breaths of pure, white energy, breathing out any negative emotions, until you start to feel relaxed.
- Be aware that you need to integrate both gold (masculine: active and decisive aspect) and silver (feminine: feeling and intuitive) energies.
- Then invoke Gabriel like this: "*Gabriel, Gabriel, Gabriel, I ask for the power of the moon and silver to flow into me, and into my heart. In love and light, love and light, love and light.*"
- Now imagine that you can take in a deep breath of the silver power of the moon.

- Breathe this deep down into your body, visualising the masculine (gold) and feminine (silver) energy balance being restored within you.
- As you breathe out say: "*I breathe a silver star around me to strengthen my powers of intuition; help me to think matters through before I act, and aid my action to be for my ultimate highest good.*"
- You may actually be able to feel this star energy around you. It's likely to last between 36 and 48 hours, after which you would need to recreate it.
- Do this exercise as often as needed to ask for Gabriel's loving assistance with intuition to balance your life actions. Always remember to thank Gabriel.

Phuel, angel lord of the waters of earth, offers water in different guises to aid you with ambition. If you have an aquamarine crystal, this brings you closer to Phuel when trying these invocations.

To power you forwards in a venture. Phuel offers you the power of water as steam to speed you onwards in a situation. Say: '*Phuel, Phuel, Phuel, please empower me with your steam energy to move this situation forward if for my highest good. In love and light, love and light, love and light.*"

To 'freeze' a situation temporarily. Call on Phuel if you need the opposite, i.e. to pause a current situation for a short time so that you can take stock and make decisions accordingly. Say: "*Phuel, Phuel, Phuel, please empower me with your ice energy to freeze this situation so that I can evaluate it for my highest good. In love and light, love and light, love and light.*"

See also page 260 for Phuel's help to calm emotions.

Balancing/enhancing your energy with the power of essential oils.

Anahita, angel of medicinal plants, says:
I provide the love that helps each plant to grow and flower, my wings lift the seeds to spread and multiply the healing opportunities. My silver energy combines this power with water of love and life to make a remedy to help heal, balance and energise your body.

Use two or three drops of a suitable oil on a small amount of water to fragrance a room while doing any of the exercises/meditations concerning the energy centres indicated in this Scorpio month. (If you are pregnant you should take further advice before using essential oils.)

Red for base of spine (energy/empowerment): Patchouli and vetivert are both grounding and strengthening.
Orange for navel area (transformation/new ideas): Neroli enhances creativity; orange is for joy; sandalwood is spiritual.
Pink (including coral pink) for the heart (including healing): Rose oil helps to connect you to the angels.
Mauve for the brow area (psychic perception): Juniper is cleansing; clary sage aids dream recall; lavender is calming, cleansing and balancing.

Ariel, angel ruler of Pluto, guides you with psychic/spiritual matters.

Safe psychic and spiritual development. The colours for this are mauve and violet and the main crystal is amethyst, as it is the link between underworld and over world and to other dimensions or realities. This crystal is connected with Ariel, angel of air. If you have an amethyst, hold or carry it while calling on Ariel's love and protection.

To call on Ariel for this help. Say: *"Ariel, Ariel, Ariel, I ask for your help in developing my psychic skills safely. Help me to channel the power of violet into my third eye, for I wish to increase my intuitive awareness to guide my self-development, for my highest good."*

See also the meditation with Ariel on page 272–3.

Angels to help you maintain your integrity in your new ventures.

Zadkiel, angel of integrity and wisdom. Zadkiel, ruler of Jupiter, aids you with maintaining your principles and integrity in difficult situations. If you feel this would help you at present, say: *"Zadkiel, Zadkiel, Zadkiel, give me the wisdom to know how to proceed with integrity in my current situation. In love and light, love and light, love and light."* Say this every day until you have overcome the difficulty.

Arad, angel of beliefs. Arad is the angel to aid you in maintaining your pure principles and ideals when tackling new ventures. If you are evaluating something and need his help, call on Arad until you have completed your evaluation, saying: *"Arad, Arad, Arad, when I make my decisions about self-development please wrap me in your wings with positive energy, so that I work only for my highest good. In love and light, love and light, love and light."*

Duma helps you find the still point within yourself, to determine your true ambitions, those that will make you happiest.

Duma's message to you:
From the void, the origin of All Life, I sweep on my golden wings. Mine is the medium of contemplation, for I can bring you, too, to your still point in the heart of your heart, the silent core of your being wherein all is known but may not be yet understood. Let me aid you to find this understanding, so that you can ask your heart about your future.

If you resonate with Duma's message, invoke him saying: *"Duma, Duma, Duma, take me into my own still point, my place of perfect peace, so that my heart can help me to make this important decision about my future. In love and light, love and light, love and light."*

Now close your eyes and breathe deeply of Duma's golden light. When you feel calm, go into this special place to see what your heart says.

Ariel, ruler of earth, air and Pluto, offers you this purple exercise for psychic skills, to help you expand your spiritual consciousness.

- Hold an amethyst crystal (if you have one), to programme this during the meditation.
- Close your eyes and start taking deep breaths of pure, white energy, breathing out any negative emotions, until you start to feel relaxed.
- Then invoke Ariel like this: *"Ariel, Ariel, Ariel, please help me to access the violet-purple ray of magic and mystery. In love and light, love and light, love and light."*
- Now imagine that you can breathe in this violet-purple light, and with each breath take it deeper into yourself, becoming filled with purple energy.
- Send it down through your feet into earth, and then upwards through your crown into air, so that you are connected to underworld and over world.
- Now send it towards your forehead (third eye chakra) as this is the psychic energy centre of the body.

🍂 Say: "Ariel, Ariel, Ariel, I ask for your guidance and your loving protection. With the purple ray, strengthen my inner knowing; help me to understand how to safely develop my psychic skills and expand my spiritual consciousness, for my highest good, highest good, highest good."

🍂 Wait for guidance from Ariel, which may come immediately or in the form of synchronicity to guide you as to what to do next.

🍂 You always have a choice as to whether or not you follow the path Ariel suggests.

🍂 Keep the crystal (if you used one) until your path is set.

Helping a beloved soul to pass

"Recently my beloved cat, Miss Doogle, became ill. Unfortunately, her illness was terminal and I brought her home to say goodbye. I immediately called on the angels as taught to me by Angela's books, 'in love and light, love and light, love and light', to come to give comfort and healing. I knew I had to let Miss Doogle go, but it was hard and I needed help. I asked that she be comforted, and I in my very humanness asked for healing. The angels knew what was required and the healing was for Miss Doogle to be without pain, and healing to fix the hole that was opening in my heart.

"The angels came – legions of them. I went from frantic, heart-wrenching sobs to a feeling of calm. I knew they were there.

"Over the next 36 or so hours, I prayed and meditated. I played healing music for Miss Doogle and talked to her. I told her how much I loved her and would miss her. I told her how many memories we had – and I thanked her for being my companion. I learnt so many lessons from her and I was thankful. Throughout those hours, I could feel the peace of the angels – it was a 'feeling' and a 'knowing', because I believed in them. I asked Raphael for healing comfort and Rachmiel for comfort during my grief.*

"On the way to the vet's office for the final appointment, during which we would help Miss Doogle to transition, I could almost 'see' the angels outside the car flying around us as we drove. They were in the car and definitely in the Quiet Room as I talked with Miss Doogle. 'Let go, my love,' I said. 'It's okay to go to the light and be reborn again. Angels are waiting to guide you to heaven. Go in peace and love.'

"When the vet was about to begin the injection, Miss Doogle lifted up her head and looked up – I knew someone had come for her. Even before the injection could get into her system, she laid her beloved head down and her spirit soared to the angels.

"Thank you, angels!"

(from Bobbi Malanowski of Dallas, Texas, USA)

[* you could also call upon Hariel, angel of tame animals, in such a circumstance (the author)]

Reaching for the sky with expansion of your personal horizons.

Adnachiel, angel ruler of Sagittarius

My golden arrow is ready to take your eye towards new and exciting horizons. I bring the marvellous possibility of expansion, through vision and action, to make your dreams come true. No matter where you are on the path of life, there is always room for self-development. First you need optimism to feed the power of vision, then you must have the determination and stamina to turn vision into reality. The pure gold fire of passion in my sign empowers these aims and my love underpins your dreams of a different life. My energy and Jupiter's deep wisdom bring abundance and clarity to these dreams, lifting them skywards, for the sky is the limit if your heart is in the venture. I give you the chance to fly with me into the blue, towards a clearer, brighter and more fulfilling future.

Sagittarius, a fire sign, is ruled by Jupiter, planet of joy and plenty. Jupiter's ruler is Zadkiel, who brings all kinds of abundance.

This, the final month of the year, is a time for looking both back and forward. Sun angels lift your spirits if this is what you need, for Sagittarius holds the chance of freedom for further self-development, and/or to build on what you achieved this year. Adnachiel shows you not only how to have the power of vision for next year but, even more importantly, how to make this vision happen. Zadkiel, ruler of Jupiter, holds you to your inner integrity, while offering abundance that you need to make things flow. Other angels guide you with this exciting prospect of expansion of your inner and outer horizons.

View the list of personal qualities opposite. Are any of these elements that you need in your life just now? The angels are always around to help you, but it is your choice as to whether or not you invite them in.

Personal qualities linked with Sagittarius and Adnachiel:

Optimism, power of vision and action, realism
Freedom for expansion of personal and
spiritual horizons

Elemental angels offer these fire strengths:

Burning away of inner blocks to
your progress
Sun power to lift your spirits in
winter

The ruling planetary angel (Zadkiel) influences:

Abundance of whatever quality you need for
your highest good

Adnachiel helps you to get started.

First, read the angelic message on pages 277 and 278 and decide whether these apply to you. If so, look at the list of words on page 279 and choose a word or phrase with which to begin. Now turn this into an invocation: *"Adnachiel, Adnachiel, Adnachiel, please help me with my (insert the words or phrase you selected, e.g. power of vision and action). In love and light, love and light, love and light."*

If you have been working through the book you will have read in earlier chapters how to hold out your hands in front of you, to learn to feel the response of the angel to your invocation.

If this is new to you, then just keep trying, because you definitely will be able to learn to feel the angel energy coming in.

As the vibration around you changes, your ears may pop slightly.

It may or may not be a bit difficult for you to feel the angel energy to begin with. Try several angelic invocations from the chapter, to get used to the idea, and to sense the difference between each angel's energy.

As you get better at doing the invocations and working with the angels, you gradually raise your own vibration nearer to the angels themselves, which in turn means that you feel their presence more when talking to them.

You will increasingly be able to sense even subtle energy. Some people start to see pictures as well, when they become proficient.

Treat the angels as your loved and trusted friends, for that is what they are.

Sahaqiel, angel of the sky, will expand your horizons skywards and even beyond.

Sahaqiel says:
Fly skyward with me on gilded wings, soaring into the celestial blue, like a golden dove seeking Father Sun. Gradually my secrets will be revealed, for the sky is the limit as your energy and enthusiasm set your spirit free. You must realise that expansion of horizons is a dual process. First, you need awareness of the physical horizon of your world, so that you can appreciate the possible scope for your activities. Only then can you truly expand your inner consciousness to meet the challenge of new horizons.

If this resonates with you, call on Sahaqiel, by saying: *"Sahaqiel, Sahaqiel, Sahaqiel, please help me to expand my view of my inner and outer horizons. I know that I have yet to realise my true life potential, but with your loving support the sky is the limit. In love and light, love and light, love and light."*

Here are two affirmations to try with Adnachiel. Remember, if you choose to make affirmations, do them as often as you can (at least daily) until you feel you are making something happen for yourself.

For more optimism about the future: *"Adnachiel, I deserve to be optimistic about my future prospects, for the time has come to let go of self-doubt and go for something that will stretch my talents and bring me a greater sense of fulfilment."*

To be realistic and focused: *"Adnachiel, I know that I need to be more than just a dreamer to expand my horizons. With your support I shall be confident and focus both on my concept of the future and on the action to bring this to fruition."*

If you need freedom because you have been stuc
certain situation for too long.

Pedael, angel of deliverance, says:
There are many ways in which you might seek deliverance. Perha
in a situation with regard to work, home or a relationship and don't
how to extricate yourself, especially if there are implications on others.
Invoke my name with loving intent and ask for guidance on ho
free, without hurting others any more than necessary. If you are prepar
to be a little patient, sending Love and Light daily to the problem in my
name, a solution will be found.

If you need his help, invoke Pedael, saying: *"Pedael, Pedael, P*
I know I need to extricate myself from this situa
a way to be free with as little hurt as possible, so that I can re-find my
vision of the future. In love and light, love and light, love and light."

Keep doing this invocation every day until things begin to resolve
themselves.

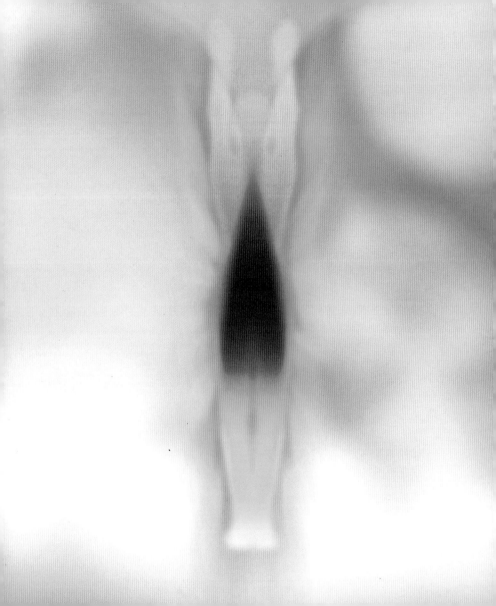

In this fire sign month, Uriel helps you with this exercise to 'burn away' something in you that holds back the expansion of your horizons.

- Let's assume that you want to expand your personal horizons, either inwardly or in your activities generally.
- First, take time to think about anything within you that holds you back from forming a vision of expansion for your future.
- Write down on a piece of paper anything you wish to change or 'burn away' within your mind, body or spirit; it might be a habit or craving, a memory, hurt or personality trait.
- Tuck the piece of paper somewhere on your person.
- Stand up and stretch your arms straight up, as far as possible above your head, then close your eyes so you can focus on what you can feel rather than what you see.
- While holding your arms up, invoke Uriel as follows: "*Uriel, Uriel, Uriel, send the cleansing and purifying fire down through my arms and into my body to rid me of (say out loud whatever you wrote). In love and light, love and light, love and light.*"
- Imagine (you may actually feel) the healing energy from fire flowing down your arms; visualise it flowing around in the area behind your stomach (solar and sacral areas), which is where your emotions are held, cleansing and balancing them.
- Tell yourself this is permanent and to reinforce your thought burn the paper, and bury the ash or wash it away.
- Thank Uriel for his help.

Colours and candle power help, in this Sagittarius month, with optimism, perception, intuition and decision-making.

For Adnachiel and Sagittarius the colours are many shades of blue, from sky blue to lapis blue, gradually deepening to purple. Gold also features in this month, as it is a fire sign.

Shades of blue deepening to purple. Paler blues help you to see your true way forward, encouraging you to reach for the sky and beyond with Sahaqiel (see page 282). Chrysocolla is a useful crystal to aid you with this. As blue becomes purple, it guides you towards your psychic and spiritual expansion path. Amethyst or ametrine would be crystals to use for this.

Sagittarius is ruled by Jupiter. Jupiter's ruler is Zadkiel, whose deep blue is flecked with gold to signify ancient wisdom. Zadkiel's lapis lazuli or turquoise are also suitable for this month. Gold also brings optimism, power of fire and sun to empower decision and action for your vision of the future.

Using candles in a fire sign month. Candles help add fire energy to exercises this month. Use a candle of this month's colours, etching the Sagittarius symbol on it (see pages 278–9), while doing an exercise.

Breathing in sun energy with Gazardiel, one of the sun angels, even in winter.

Gazardiel's message to you:
My task is to ensure that the sun completes its daily path without which life could not be sustained on the surface of Mother Earth. This daily miracle ensures the sun's power is felt whatever the season. Even when the fire of the sun is hidden from you, you can still bring its power of optimism into body and mind by invoking my aid.

To reinforce Gazardiel's message you could also do the exercise on page 290.

Gazardiel, a sun angel, offers a bowl of sunlight for optimism, if you feel your energy is depleted due to lack of sunshine in the winter months.

- Imagine that in front of you there is an invisible bowl of yellow fire, representing the sun, that you can hold in your hands.
- Take three deep breaths of this shining yellow light, ensuring that you breathe it right down into your body and that you *will* it to help you.
- Focus on your solar plexus in particular, which is the seat of the sun within you and the area where your emotions are stored.
- With your will, visualise this whole area of your body becoming golden as your own sun ignites within you.
- Dark thoughts are banished as you let invisible sunlight fill you with new vigour and optimism.
- Gazardiel says: *"I, Gazardiel, aid you to lock in this benefit with the power of love and light."*
- Remember to thank Gazardiel. Do this exercise as often as you need to during the winter to lift your spirits.

Sandalphon's guidance on a path of spiritual self-development.

Sandalphon, angel of prayer, says:
I guide your way on the shining silver path of your personal spiritual development. Call my name as you pray. I gather your prayers as soon as you form them whether in mind or with speech, and I turn them to flowers of radiant purity as I convey them to heaven on your behalf.

To invoke Sandalphon, say: *"Sandalphon, Sandalphon, Sandalphon, please convey my prayers and give me guidance to understand fully the messages I receive in return, for I wish to make spiritual progress. In love and light, love and light, love and light."*

Oriel, angel of destiny, clarifies your vision. Say: *"Oriel, Oriel, Oriel, I seek my true destiny in life and ask for your loving support with my vision, as I work with you and Isiaiel towards a more fulfilling future. In love and light, love and light, love and light."*

Isiaiel is the golden guardian angel of the future.

Isiaiel's message:

On rays as fine as gleaming golden thread I weave the complex pattern of your future. To create a harmonious and colourful pattern let us work together. First, we need to address your vision and ensure it is realistic, as this is the key. It is the first part of the pattern, for with this in place we can focus on the necessary action. If you need my aid you can invoke me, and together we can begin to weave for you a wonderful, inspired and colourful design.

To re-pattern your future, call on Isiaiel as follows: *"Isiaiel, Isiaiel, Isiaiel, please be with me now to re-create the pattern of my life. I let go of the past and look towards a better future, one in which I am inspired to expand my personal horizons, for my highest good, highest good, highest good."*

Isiaiel offers angelic coaching for a better future on pages 294–5.

Isiaiel coaches you on how to work towards setting goals for expansion of your inner self or activities.

To determine your new goals. Take a piece of paper. Sit down and think for a little while about your life and what you would really like to be doing if you could choose. To help you focus, invoke Isiaiel: *"Isiaiel, Isiaiel, Isiaiel, please help me to determine my self-development aspirations and decide what it is I really want to do in my life, for my own highest good. In love and light, love and light, love and light."*

In your heart you know the answer. Write down your perceived goal on the piece of paper.

To identify what is stopping you doing this. Say: *"Isiaiel, Isiaiel, Isiaiel, please help me to clarify exactly what is preventing me from doing what I want to do or achieving what I should like to achieve in future. In love and light, love and light, love and light."*

There may be several obstacles in your way. Carefully list all the things that are stopping you from progressing towards your goal.

How could you deal with these obstacles? Focus on each obstacle and let Isiaiel guide your heart about what to do. Say: *"Isiaiel, Isiaiel, Isiaiel, please be with me now to give guidance on how I could overcome each of these obstacles, for my highest good, highest good, highest good."*

Now begin to write an action plan for yourself. Against each obstacle write down how you can deal with it, so that one by one they will disappear.

You can now move forward. Say: *"Isiaiel, Isiaiel, Isiaiel, please guide me with my action plan, setting realistic dates by when I can overcome the obstacles. By doing this I am clearing my path for future happiness. In love and light, love and light, love and light."*

Keep working on this, reviewing your plan as often as necessary. Your future is in your own hands, but you can always be supported by the angels.

Breathing a lapis blue and gold star around you with Zadkiel, ruler of Jupiter, to aid abundance of vision, optimism and opportunity.

- Hold a lapis lazuli crystal, if you have one, in your left hand.
- Close your eyes and begin taking deep breaths of pure, white energy, breathing out any negative emotions, until you start to feel relaxed.
- Now, invoke Zadkiel: *"Zadkiel, Zadkiel, Zadkiel, I ask for your power, the power of Jupiter, to flow into me, to allow me to receive the abundance I deserve. In love and light, love and light, love and light."*
- Imagine that you are taking in deep breaths of blue and gold.
- Breathe these colours down and allow them to permeate throughout your body.
- Feel yourself become completely filled with Zadkiel's abundance.

🕭 As you breathe out, say: "*I breathe a deep blue star around me, sparkling with the gold of wisdom, to help me to recognise the abundance opportunity I need. Let the Universe bring me this abundance, for my highest good, and I undertake to share it with others.*"

🕭 Whilst connected to Zadkiel's energy, focus your mind on the specific kind of abundance you are requesting; mentally send the message to Zadkiel.

🕭 You may actually be able to feel this star energy around you. If you can't, don't worry, as it's still there and should last for about 36–48 hours.

🕭 If you held a crystal, you programmed it with your request, so carry it around to keep the crystal energy with you all the time.

🕭 Always remember to thank the angels for their help.

Experiencing the energy of the angels

Throughout this book you have seen how I suggest invoking angels daily to enrich, transform and guide your life. This can bring truly amazing results – you just need to do it with love and trust for special things to begin to happen. To conclude my book advising you to call on an Angel for Every Day, here is a personal account of what happens when she selects a card from the 144 Gold, Silver & Balance Guardian Angel Cards – something she does every time she walks past them. May wonderful things happen to you, too.

"Adorning the environment of my spacious living room is a bowl filled with exquisitely coloured crystals. Within this bowl are placed the Gold & Silver Guardian Angel card decks along with the Balance card deck. Every time I walk past the bowl my hand reaches over; for a moment in time and space I receive words of guidance, truth and revelation.

"Having traversed the threshold of the Path of Return, Metatron fills my peripheral vision with silvery-white sparks against a backdrop of Michael's horizon filled with opaque oceans of blue. The colours vibrate, merge and blend as I am fulfilling my everyday tasks. The vision of these intermingling colours lights up my path each step of the way. My mortal vision is dark, as I journey through the birthing portal towards enlightenment and revelation.

"Placed within the womb of Metatron's divine guidance and sustenance, I am floating like a child, once again regaining a momentum of purity and connection to the Divine Intention, as it seeks to move in and through my life to propel me towards the fulfilment of my true destiny.

"Pistis Sophia sets my heart centre aglow with golden light and surrounds the outline of my body with silver. My spiritual heart is alive, surging with life force, emitting sparks of celestial stars as the connection with my head begins to occur. My spine tingles as I surrender to the divine surgery taking place upon my Soul, allowing me to reclaim access to who and what I truly AM.

"Overwhelming waves of blessings overtake my being. Pulsating, vibrating, nurturing sustenance of light tantalizes my taste buds as I begin to savour the new life I have so longed to experience consciously while my feet are walking upon the earth.

"Silvery-white angel wings now form before my eyes as my story draws to an end."

(from Antonella Celi, Rosebud, Victoria, Australia)

Index

Acknowledgements

This book is, as ever, for my wonderfully supportive family. It's also for my friends and for those loyal readers (whose emails are so appreciated) who have been asking for a practical handbook, so that they can really start to live life every day in the company of angels. My thanks go, as always, to all at my publishers, Quadrille, who helped to bring this book to fruition, and to Anne Furniss, my editor, and to Richard Rockwood for his ever-more-amazing artworks. And finally, once again, to the angels, who continue to inspire me every single day. What a wonderful world! I would also like to thank all those who offered their personal stories of connections with the angels for inclusion in the book: Antonella Celi, Nancy Alvarado, Rachel Durnford, Michelle Esclapez, Katalyn Feijens, Vicki Grady, Alison Greensmith, Alison Joy Kyle, Bobbi Malanowski, Wei Tang Phillips, Leitia Ravenscroft, Dympna Swan, Dagmar Walker and Jackie Wheatley.

Author's website: www.angelamcgerr.com
The CD Angelic *Meditations for Harmony and Balance* (see page 251) is available from the author's website or from www.harmonyhealing.co.uk

Gold and silver sun and moon garden on pages 178–9
I would like to thank my sister, Fiona Stephenson, for allowing us to feature her design for this garden. Anyone who wishes to use this design and plant the garden should contact her at
Fiona Stephenson Designs
www.fionastephensondesigns.com
emails: info@fionastephensondesigns.com

Angel meditation bags
Anyone interested in buying Leitia Ravenscroft's Angel Meditation Bags (see page 154) can contact her at ambient3@hotmail.co.uk.